T0362967

PUBLISHED BY BOOM BOOKS

www.boombooks.biz

ABOUT THIS SERIES

.... But after that, I realised that I knew very little about these parents of mine. They had been born about the start of the Twentieth Century, and they died in 1970 and 1980. For their last 50 years, I was old enough to speak with a bit of sense.

I could have talked to them a lot about their lives. I could have found out about the times they lived in. But I did not. I know almost nothing about them really. Their courtship? Working in the pits? The Lock-out in the Depression? Losing their second child? Being dusted as a miner? The shootings at Rothbury? My uncles killed in the War? Love on the dole? There were hundreds, thousands of questions that I would now like to ask them. But, alas, I can't. It's too late.

Thus, prompted by my guilt, I resolved to write these books. They describe happenings that affected people, real people. The whole series is, to coin a modern phrase, designed to push your buttons, to make you remember and wonder at things forgotten.

The books might just let nostalgia see the light of day, so that oldies and youngies will talk about the past and re-discover a heritage otherwise forgotten. Hopefully, they will spark discussions between generations, and foster the asking and answering of questions that should not remain unanswered.

BORN IN 1961

WHAT ELSE HAPPENED?

RON WILLIAMS

AUSTRALIAN SOCIAL HISTORY

BOOK 23 IN A SERIES OF 34

FROM 1939 TO 1972

BOOM, BOOM BABY, BOOM

BORN IN 1961? WHAT ELSE HAPPENED?

Published by Boom Books. Wickham, NSW, Australia

Web: boombooks.biz

Email: email@boombooks.biz

Title: Born in 1961? What else happened? Ron Williams

ISBN: 97809648771654

Cover images: National Archives of Australia A1200, L40593, Miss Australia 1961, Tania Verstak; A1200, L39492, playwright at home; A12111, 11/1961/21/9, family backyard; A1501, A2759/1, TV cameraman at work.

TABLE OF CONTENTS

IMPORTANT PEOPLE AND EVENTS

Australian Prime Minister	**Bob Menzies**
Opposition Leader	**Arthur Calwell**
Governor General	**Vis+ Dunrossil**
.... From August 3rd	**Viscount De L'Isle**
British Monarch	**Queen Elizabeth**
British Prime Minister	**Harold McMillan**
The Pope	**John XXIII**
US President	**John Kennedy**
Australian cricket captain	**Richard Benaud**

MELBOURNE CUP

1960	**Hi Jinx**
1961	**Lord Fury**
1962	**Even Stevens**

THE ASHES

1958 - 59	**Australia 4 - 1**
1961	**Drawn 2 - 2**
1962 - 63	**England 3 - 1**

ACADEMY AWARDS

Best Actor	**Max Schell**
Best Actress	**Sophia Lauren**

THOUGHTS FROM 1960

The world had seen a lot of tough times in the last twenty years. Firstly, there were the dreadful seven years of the wars in Europe and the Asia-Pacific. That was a period marred by thoughts and reality of death, of long-term separation from loved ones, of austerity and rationing, and of **repression of freedoms for the common good**.

This was followed by a battle, for half a decade, to kick the War habit. There was diminishing need for austerity, rationing could be relaxed, regulations and constraints could be lifted. The world was a better place, a safer place, but still there was the shadow of the dreadful War years haunting many lives.

As well, there were the many kill-joys in high positions who had enjoyed the power that war had given them, and **who stood firmly in the way of returning to normal**. Thus, for example, butter rationing continued till 1949, and petrol rationing till 1950. Price controls on rents, and on most goods and services, on banking, on imports, on what-have-you, were still very evident. Still, there were no blackouts, nor tank traps on the beaches, and it was all much, much better than war. Though, as a young lad, I did miss the searchlights at night.

The fun started in the Fifties. After Bob Menzies got his title of Prime Minister back, the Baby Boomers took over. This horde of revellers were now having their second child, starting to build a house in the developing housing estates on the fringes of cities, and buying a car on hire purchase. Hills Hoist sales were booming, jobs were easy to get in most years, electric lawn-mowers could be afforded, and everyone by now had a 40-hour week. So life was good and getting better. In top of that, the decade saw the embarrassment of a few Tall Poppies, like Dr Evatt in the Petrov Case, and Bob Menzies in the Suez Affair. What more could you ask?

So, here we are in the Sixties. The year 1960 was marred by some serious events. The kidnap and killing of Sydney schoolboy Graeme Thorne was a national tragedy, and brought home to the population that kidnapping was not just an American or overseas threat, but that it could happen here as well. **No one could believe that**.

Then there were the killings of South Africans in Sharpville, and the many arguments that Australia faced a similar situation in New Guinea. Also, a man and wife were found murdered in Maitland, and both heads were missing. The head of the wife was found a week later floating in Newcastle Harbour, and her mother was called to identify it. This was gruesome stuff.

But we had some lighter scenes as well. The Russian Premier, Nikita Khrushchev, went to the United Nations, and at the end of a Session, took off his shoe and belted the rostrum as he spoke and shouted for ten minutes. An American temperance expert got a lot of publicity when he said Australian women were drunks. They were defended by an equally illustrious Australian gentleman who said "Australian alcoholic women tend to be wardrobe drinkers. They rarely appear drunk in public." Some people wondered whether this really was much of a defence.

Jack Kramer made his first real deal in Oz, to allow professional tennis. Princess Margaret and her boyfriend

Anthony Armstrong-Jones had a confused period that ended in their getting married, and self-service petrol pumps were the subject of much controversy. Finally, the bandicoots, with their fleas, were being very irritating in some areas of Sydney, and the Letter writers to the newspapers were vocal for "something to be done about them." To me, this plague seemed trivial. And so it was I suppose, but it was **a lucky country** that **thought** it serious enough to get upset about.

MORE NEWS FROM 1960: THE COLD WAR

In 1960, the Cold War was at one of its high points. This meant the USA and the USSR were each doing their best to get other nations of the world to join their camp in the ideological war of Capitalism versus Communism. At a lesser level, it meant that each country would promote revolutions, strikes, protests, assassinations, and dissension wherever they thought it advantageous to themselves. They also handed out large sums of money to the smaller nations, and vast supplies of armaments.

At the same time, each kept up a propaganda war aimed at proving that **it** was blameless, that **its** policies were always right, that **the other party really was a baddie**, and that it had the military might to squash anyone who got it really annoyed. It was all very silly.

Here in Australia we were on the side of America. That means that every day our papers were full of news, real or imagined, compiled by US agencies, that told us the good stuff that America was doing, and that our side was slowly but surely winning. At the same time, internally within

Australia, the local Reds were taking a constant beating from the Liberals, especially Bob Menzies.

If I wanted to, I could fill this book with all of these antics. But, like most of the population at the time, I had tired of them. All the bluster, the threats, and justifications had been heard hundreds of times, and become ho-hum. So, I will not dwell on them. Here and there throughout this book, I will mention the Cold War and its consequences, but discussion of it will generally be limited. But you should keep in mind, occasionally, that **the Cold War was in fact everywhere**, and that it was, one way or another, a major force behind many of the world's events and philosophies at that time.

DECIMAL CURRENCY IS GETTING NEAR

Letters, A Erickson. What is needed is not a conversion of the monetary system to decimals, but complete eradication of the decimal system in favour of a system of counting in dozens – may we be preserved from that nasty word duodecimal!

As Mr Sinclair so rightly pointed out, the advantages of this system, with it easy divisibility, are boundless. With a little mental effort, some practice, and the addition of a few new symbols and words to the language (we already have twelve, dozen and gross), the arithmetical processes become no more difficult than they are with a decimal system. Surely by now we have advanced sufficiently from our primitive state to be able to do our counting without recourse to fingers and toes.

Letters, C Sullivan. Mr Sinclair's   flippant championing of "the dozen" reminds me that this awkward numeral was introduced into England by the Vikings in the barbaric past, and the Danes I have informed of this fact were incredulous, as they have been on the decimal system a long time. Most of them thought that it was a very good joke indeed at our expense.

Even the once backward countries of Russia, India and China have adopted the decimal system entirely and not only for currency as Australian advocates propose.   Outside of Britain and Ireland, the only important countries not using decimal currency are Australia and New Zealand. According to Mr Sinclair, the rest are all "oot of step but oor Jock."

Letters, S Goard. Will C Sullivan consider the following contra points flippant?

Changing to decimal currency will: be a break with the UK; will cost over 30 million Pounds of public expenditure (not to consider private incidentals); will increase the prices of a great many small household items and services; will upset wool market bidding (which runs to farthings); will end the liaison 'twixt pence and dozens, pence and inches (12 to a ---); will abolish the dual facility of thirds and quarters of the basic coin; and will complicate interest workings, which are so simple. Is it worth it all – merely to follow suit? If any advantages, they are doubtless to a small section in "big business."

NEW AUSTRALIANS

Migrants were still pouring into the country, and were being assimilated, more or less. Of course, they were all from Europe, because in Asia we were still in the post-War stage of never the twain shall meet. Anyway, these new arrivals were often described as "New Australians". To many people, this was more respectful than pommy or geordie, dago, or wop. Mr Menzies, anticipating by 50 years the current vogue for political correctness, thought this new term was altogether too demeaning, and looked forward to its demise. This started a little controversy in the Letters Columns.

Letters, Geoff Cahill. Surely Mr Cahill must realise that a number of these fine people were and are nationals of many old countries forced by uncontrollable political circumstances to migrate, thus leaving all of those valued family and national ties which are not easily forgotten in a short space of time?

This is of course Australia's gain but, until naturalised, why can't they be accorded the basic courtesy of referring to them by their nationality, such as "Austrian", "Polish", etc?

Letters, Donald Mackay. Mr Calwell, during his term as Minister for Immigration, made a plea for the introduction of "New Australian" to replace the harsher "refugee" and "displaced person". The term was widely accepted both officially and unofficially and the alternative terms virtually disappeared. Now, this eminently sensible and realistic term is under fire.

While a changing language is often inspired by a healthy desire for greater precision, some changes are made with no apparent object other than to dilute realism and colour. New Australians are literally new Australians, and I have yet to meet one who resented being called just that. Let us not allow a change to something which would be less accurate and less meaningful.

Letters, F Krynen. Mr Donald Mackay mentions that he has yet to meet an immigrant who resented being call a "New Australian". The term "New Australian" is patronising to the utmost degree.

Although I have resided in Australia now for 12 years and have been a British subject for seven years, I am still occasionally called a "New Australian", possibly because of my slight accent. I always was, and still am, extremely proud of being born in Holland. After all, every Australian was a foreigner to me. Seven years ago I pledged my loyalty to our Queen and country. I am an Australian (not by accident, but by choice), a fact of which I am very proud, and I resent being called anything else.

Letters, Spartacus. I resent the expression "New Australian"; I resent it deeply. I was naturalised in 1949; every time I am still called "New Australian" I am asking myself whether I made a mistake by applying for naturalisation. As long as the term "New Australian" is generally and officially accepted, naturalisation looks like a hypocritical and dishonest farce. Those "many thousand migrants" who prefer to maintain their original citizenship as full and first-class citizens of their country of origin are fully justified.

Comment. What other term could be used. One person wants to be called a Dutchman, and the other wants "Australian". Then again, there are those who do not want to be labelled at all.

Letters, Jon the Frog. I object to all of the terms suggested. I do not want to be know by dago, or Australian, or French, or anything. My name is Jon. I want to be known as Jon. Nothing else.

Comment. I came from a coal-mining community, and over half the men there were Poms. They prided themselves on being described as such. Half a dozen of them were nick-named "Geordie" and again they revelled in this. It was not the terminology that mattered. It was the intent that went with it. I suspect that it was this that rankled with some people.

Second comment. The term "New Australian" took decades to die out. I note that young people in the 2020's do not use it, and tend towards the person's original nationality. Of course, some people of my generation still do it unconsciously, though not in any way patronising or derogatory. At the same time, **naturalisation** is no longer the big issue that it was in 1961. I recently asked a 24-year old graduate, in talking about foreign students, "does naturalisation loom large in your thinking?" and she replied "what's that?"

EXPECTATIONS OF 1961

The *Sun Herald* Editor on January 1st summed up the views of the nation's leading newspapers with the words "a year ago the new decade opened in a blaze of optimism. Nowhere was that optimism brighter than in Australia. **Events have not justified this optimism.** The first year of the sixties has been one of frustration, disappointment and crisis, at home and abroad."

He goes on to say that our overseas markets were becoming more competitive, that inflation remained a problem and that the nation was still suffering from too many strikes. On the international front, there were a number of hot spots that threatened stability.

He went on to mention Laos, the Belgian Congo, Indonesia, and Algeria, all of which we will return to as their problems persist. Cuba was worthy of special mention because of increasing reports that the US would soon invade that country, and oust Castro as leader. Of course, at this stage, that was all paper-talk, because the incoming US President, John Kennedy, would want to assess the situation himself, and decide on his own polices. That should take some time.

The Editor went on to conclude "the task which confronts us in 1961 is not to make our individual lives more comfortable. In the face of challenges, we may the more quickly find the incentives for the hard work and sacrifice which alone can give us peace and prosperity."

Comment. All the Editorials on that day ended with a similar admonition. Be sensible, look out for pitfalls, work harder, save more, be conservative. Steady up a bit. The trouble was that the Oz people were in no mood to do this. They were feeling good. Employment was high, wages were adequate, the kids were generally healthy, the lawnmower was working, and the pubs had enough beer.

Also, at this time, it was the middle of the festive season, and most of the nation would be operating at half pace until the kids went back to school in February. It is too hard to get enthusiastic about the call to work harder and sacrifice more.

MY RULES IN WRITING

NOTE. Throughout this book, I rely a lot on re-producing Letters from the newspapers. Whenever I do this, I put the text in a different font, and indent it a little, and make the font somewhat smaller. **I do not edit the text at all**. That is, I do not correct spelling or grammar, and if the text gets at all garbled, I do not change it. It's just as it was seen in the Papers.

SECOND NOTE. The material for this book that comes from newspapers is reported as it was seen at the time. If the benefit of hindsight over the years changes things, then I **might** record that in my **Comments**. The info reported thus reflects matters **as they were read in 1961.**

THIRD NOTE. Let me also apologise in advance to anyone I might offend. In a work such as this, it is certain some people will think I got some things wrong. I am sure that I did, but please remember, all of this is **only my opinion**. And really, **my opinion does not matter one little bit in the scheme of things. I hope you will say "silly old bugger", shrug your shoulders, and read on.**

JANUARY: INAUGURATION OF KENNEDY

On January 22nd John Kennedy was inaugurated as President of the US. The normal fanfare and ceremony was indulged in, and the new President made the usual speech. He said that poverty would be diminished, that the rights of people would be respected, and that prosperity was just round the corner. Internationally, he spoke of a few troublesome regions and said, as usual that America was incredibly tough and ready for action, but that it did want peace and would work hard to achieve it.

If all of that was very ho-hum, the mood in America was not. People were generally very enthusiastic about the new President and his beautiful wife, and believed that the US might be entering into a new era. Somehow the nation seemed to be on the verge of peace and prosperity, and it only took one man and woman to change the archaic machinery that had made the US into a rather dreary place. For America, and for the western world, it was a day of excitement when all sense of reality was forgotten, and new dreams and hopes filled the minds of people everywhere.

HARRY MESSEL'S MESSAGE

Harry Messel had been the Professor of Physics at Sydney University for nine years. While there he founded the Nuclear Research Foundation. Born in Canada, he had a reputation as a great publicist for physics and a great fund-raiser for the Foundation. This was a period when science was regarded as the potential solution to all the problems of the world. Among the sciences, nuclear physics was highest of all. So, for a few years, when Messel spoke, people listened.

On January 5th he spoke out on student failures at University level. He argued that 85 per cent of failures at university were caused by student laziness. He advocated a change in university policy so that after **a single** failure a student would be thrown out. The current policy was to **allow two failures and then ask the student** if he could explain himself. Messel's proposal was a very radical one. Not everyone agreed with him.

Responses to Letters varied from the thoroughly contemptuous retort of Abigail Connors down to more considered replies.

Letters, Abigail Connors. Professor Messel is at it again. Anything for a headline. All he has to do is make some outrageous statement and you and the other newspapers will propagate it. The Professor would be well advised to go count his atoms, and leave the analysis of education results to people who are expert in the matter.

Letters, Peter Wilson, Sydney University. We are asked to accept on faith Professor Messel's figure of 85 per cent. This completely ignores all the significant research work **which has failed to incriminate student laziness** as the major factor in the failure rate. Much research work on student failures still needs to be done, but critics of the university would be well advised to at least read the research that has been done, before conjuring up solutions out of the air.

Letters, Ben Selinger, SU Science Association, Sydney. Professor Messel's publicity-provoking statement that the failure in physics is due to student laziness is an assumption made without any "scientific" basis. In contrast, I wish to present some facts which can be supported by statistical evidence.

The result of a survey, carried out by Sydney University science students, has measured student opinion on the help provided by the staff of the various departments in the Faculty of Science. In both first and second years, the Physics Department is considered by the students to be by far the most **unhelpfu**l.

Perhaps the high failure rate in Physics lies not so much in student laziness but in the failure of the Department to give students all the help they need.

Letters, G Bassett, Professor of Education, University of Queensland. If the students in the Department of Physics at Sydney University are lazy, and are failing in their studies because of this, they must be the only group of students in the university with this peculiar attitude to their studies. My experience with students would lead me to think that they have a serious, anxious, attitude to work.

These sweeping "explanations" of students' failure do a great deal of harm by confusing the public, and by diverting attention away from the need to search for the correct explanation. Coming from a scientist of such repute, these statements would appear to have a great deal of authority. It is always dangerous when a man whose authority is gained in one field makes pronouncements in another, particularly when he is a scientist who throws overboard his scientific caution in the process.

Letters, Dr Tony Madigan, St Pauls College, University of Sydney. I wish to challenge his thesis that laziness is the prime cause of first-year failure. On the whole, the 200 undergraduates in my own college last year worked harder and more consistently than did similar groups of my own generation. Before any solution to this problem will emerge, the following major factors should to be considered:

Many of the students have not studied Physics in school. They come to the University to study medicine, say, and realise that they must pass Physics I. That means they have to cover all of high school physics in one year together with the extra University content. To make this at all possible, lectures should be presented over four terms instead of three.

Then there is the fact that second year Physics classes can hold only 50 per cent of the number of first year students. That means that **50 per cent must fail**. That is sometimes stated as a sort of joke, but it is true of first year physics.

As well, most physics teachers are absolutely dreadful. They are chosen in the first place because of their knowledge of the subject, and not for their teaching ability. To make matters worse, these reluctant teachers are so superior, being expert in this subject. They despise their students, and hate having to spend a few hours per week lecturing them.

Finally, there is the normal problems of children leaving school and finding their way in an adult world.   Girls, or boys, are there for the taking, beer is plentiful, sport and other activities are freely available. And many people are living away from home, or travelling long distances.

The problem is highly complex, and just making up figures does not help.   It would now be refreshing to have attention given to the work of the experts who have, for some years, been carrying out research into its many implications.

Personal comment. I did first year physics at University a few years before Messel. I had done Physics at high school, and got a good pass in it in the LC. So for me, first year was a bludge.

As Doctor Madigan said, there were lots of students who had no physics at high school, and compared to these, students like me were clearly bound to pass. But for the other strugglers, it was immensely hard. I had a lab partner whose family offered me free board and lodgings if I would coach their son a few hours each week, and another family that offered their family holiday home at Manly for six weeks in the year. In summary, I think Messel might well have kept his opinions to himself.

MENZIES SALES TAX BACKDOWN

Australia's economy was weakening quickly. Back in November, Menzies, as Prime Minister, and Holt, his Treasurer, decided that Oz was enjoying itself too much and spending more than it should. So they brought down a series of measures aimed at slowing the economy, and these included a squeeze on borrowing from the banks and Hire Purchase Companies, and a big sales tax on the purchase of motor vehicles.

Over Christmas, sales of all things were buoyant, as they usually are. But, at this time, the bad news started to arrive. At that time, GMH announced that it was sacking 2,623 workers. It said that its sales were down as much as 46 per cent on the boom months two years ago, and down 16 per cent on a year ago. It pointed out that there was a big flow-on to other industries and that, for example, tyre and painting companies would also be laying off workers soon. Other car manufacturers then spoke out, and it appeared that between them they had sacked over 4,000 workers, and clearly worse was yet to come.

All sorts of suspicions were raised by these sackings and the stats. Could it be that their dramatic release was a political move aimed at pressuring the Government into removing the tax? Or was it a fact that the economy had been on a binge, and needed to have the brakes applied? Let's see what the Letter-writers thought.

Letters, R Oser. It is to be hoped that the Federal Government will not be intimidated by the possible effects of the decision by General

Motors-Holden's Limited to dismiss some 2,600 employees.

It is also to be deplored that this company should stoop to such measures in an obvious attempt to embarrass the Government's action to increase sales-tax on motor vehicles to the extent where it may be unavoidable for political reasons to maintain the present rate of sales-tax.

With regard to the recent economic measures on the whole, it must be remembered that it will be some time before their final effect can be gauged throughout the economy. When that time comes many loud-mouthed critics may be forced to hide their heads in shame. A good hiding spot would be behind an elementary textbook on economics.

Letters, M Rathbone. Shallow thinkers blame the Federal Government for the present debacle in the motor trade. Perhaps the credit squeeze has had some effect, but the whole issue lies deeper than that. Colossal motor car production has been conduced by the scarcity and inefficiency of transport as provided by the State Government, at the expense of the taxpayer. **Thus people have been forced to buy cars** which they could hardly afford, and to drive them on roads which are already saturated with traffic.

If all transport was handed over to efficient, profit yielding enterprise, we would have improvements in all the services, and many cars would be left at home instead of being driven into the city every day and night.

The stemming of motor car manufacture had to come sooner or later, in the name of economy, and for the sake of public safety and convenience. But the fact remains that people have to be carried backward and forward, and the solution to the whole problem seems to lie in the hands of the Labor party in general, and the State Government in particular.

Letters, W Berkman. The newspapers have made headlines of GM-H and other motor manufacturers' layoffs. These figures are spectacular, but the layoff in labour in radio and TV firms, electrical appliance manufacturers, and other consumer goods manufacturers though only 10, 50 or a few hundred at each plant must amount to a much more spectacular figure than the motor trade's. We in the retail trade can get the picture much more quickly than the politicians and the government's economic theorists in their ivory towers.

Without **adequate finance for time-payment sales**, the local manufacture of consumer goods cannot continue economically. What earthly good can this policy do our overseas trade balances?

Letters, Peter Kelly. Most of us, in our jobs and clubs and pubs, see what we reckon is a lot of money about. We get the impression Australia is pretty prosperous. Then the economists and our leaders scare the daylights out of everybody, not by telling us much that means anything to us in plain words, but by actions that sack people from their jobs and tie up credit for almost everybody else who, just the day before, were feeling that things were going along pretty well.

It may stagger the Government to know that quite a few ordinary working folk would **have preferred to see an increase in taxation to** drain off some of our so-called surplus spending power, rather than that people lose their jobs.

The Government clearly had its supporters and its critics. But this was an opportunity to Yank-bash as well, because the two biggest car producers were American Companies, Ford and General Motors. Was this in fact really a dispute about who is to run Australia, our Government or the US?

Mr Bavin and Mrs Bligh had their thoughts.

Letters, J Bavin. We are, of course, enjoying the results of having Australia turned into a battleground by two American industrial giants. Not one share in either is held in Australia, and, having elected to favour us with a close-up view of "big business" in action, they are both annoyed to find that the market for which they competed is simply not big enough – certainly not big enough to sustain a dividend rate of 425 per cent. The same thought had occurred before to less keen financial brains.

But do they seek to ameliorate the lot of the dismissed employees by a reduction in price? That doesn't seem to have occurred to anyone. Or could the dividend rate be at least temporarily cut, say, to 400 per cent?

That mightn't go down too well in Detroit or New York. It's easier, after all, to lay off some Australian workmen. Then people will join a campaign to blackguard an Australian Government elected to manage Australian affairs. The sympathy that everyone feels for the employees is none the less real because their plight appears to be unnecessary.

Letters, Amanda Bligh. It pains me to see the Australian Government under subtle attack from American car giants. This is not just a case of their profit expectations being dinted, it is about control.

Our Government says we will raise sales taxes, and the Americans say that we cannot do that and that we will have to do as they say. I do not wish to kick these companies out of Australia, because we need their capital, but if they think that they can control our Government, then we might **have** to use our boot.

Whatever the merits of the case, the statistics gradually got worse. New car sales fell from 32,000 in November to 16,000 by the end of January. Even allowing for seasonal variations, this is a huge fall. But Treasurer Holt refused to budge. On the 21st, he was adamant. "The current squeeze is necessary for the Government to achieve its objectives. I don't deny that there are people who are apprehensive about the future. All I can do is tell you that the situation will worsen before it improves." Well, that was that, it seemed. No relief.

But wait a minute. Mr Menzies was going overseas on the very next day. He was to visit Washington and London, both places where he loved to frolic. He announced that the **sales tax increases would no longer apply**, and that most of the other proposed restrictive measures would be modified by Holt in his absence. Thereupon, he boarded the plane and, for him, there was no immediate political fall-out.

Of course, this was a major backdown by the Government. The egg-covered Mr Holt was left with a difficult situation. He took a bland approach and harped on the new measures as being necessary to meet the Government's targets, and claimed that the relaxations showed how the economy was constantly changing, and that policy needed to respond at an equal pace.

In the long run, the whole incident inspired little confidence in the management ability of the Liberals, and **was remembered by many in the elections** held at the end of the year. **You can bet that the three writers below had not forgotten at election-time.**

Letters, Keith McKenzie. Australians are living beyond their means and the Government rightly assessed that the motor industry, aided by hire-purchase companies, was largely responsible for our extravagance. Why didn't the Government stick to its guns and thus cause more money to be channelled into the export industries? This will have to be done if Australia is to avoid international bankruptcy.

In America, Britain, Canada and France, car-makers have had to slacken production because the world has an over-production of cars. Surely the local industry should be prepared to accept its share of the lessened demand without wielding a big stick to beat the Government into submission.

Letters, F Smith. It appears to me that the Commonwealth Government is under a definite obligation **to rebate the 10 per cent increase** in sales-tax paid by purchasers of cars within the **November 15 – February period**.

The increase in tax, together with credit restrictions, was an emergency measure introduced by the Commonwealth Government solely as a means of curbing that section of industry, namely the manufacturing and selling of motor cars, which was one of the main causes of upset to the economy. The aim was to stop people buying motor cars. In this they were very successful. And from the resulting unemployment possibly a little more successful than they bargained for, **hence the rather sudden decision to revert to the old tax rate**.

In view of the Prime Minister's statement that the extra sales-tax was not introduced for revenue purposes but as a deterrent only, and now that this aim has been more than achieved, it is most unfair that those people who were forced through necessity to pay the higher tax should be penalised.

Now that the unbalanced situation in the motor industry has been corrected, there is no reason that I can see why the purchasers of motor vehicles within this period should not have the extra tax refunded. As one of the unfortunates who purchased a vehicle within this period my views are, of necessity, rather biased, but if the extra tax was not required for revenue purposes it belongs in the pockets of the purchasers.

Letters, K Garland.   I am in full agreement with J Walker How long are we going to have to put up with this sort of situation? I charge the Government with (a) being incapable of handling the affairs of our nation, and (b) keeping in its employ advisers who are either socialists in their thinking or have not the slightest knowledge of business principles.

The lifting of import controls with the subsequent flooding of the market **by the same merchandise as is produced here** shows a lack of commonsense that is beyond my reasoning.

Comment. Menzies' political situation was pretty weak. His Liberal Party, combined with the Country Party, held enough seats to allow them to govern. But his power was based on two factors.

The first was his never-ending anti-Communism. Every time he needed votes he got on this band-wagon, and the community came to his rescue. Remember, the Cold War was at a peak, so to push the **Reds under the Beds** theme always alarmed some people, and they clung to him for safety.

Secondly, he had held office now for 10 years straight, and most of the time, the national economy had been good. In fact, there had been a couple of booms that brought general prosperity. So, in these easy years, he had built himself a reputation as a stable and sound manager of the economy.

Now that things were toughening up a lot, he needed to keep this record intact.   Right now, after this sales-tax debacle, he **looked like a dunce** to many.

THE GOVERNOR GENERAL

Viscount Dunrossil had been Governor General of Australia for only a year when he suddenly died in his sleep. Australians generally had not had a chance to know him well, but what they saw was enough to convince them that he was a good and fair man, who was quite prepared to carry out his duties in a manner befitting.

By the end of January, attention was passing to the person who might replace him. Mr Menzies, of course, with his strong affiliation to the Queen and all things British, would certainly want some distinguished Englishman who would have no connection to Australian politics. On the other hand, the Labor Party wanted an Australian. The trouble was that most distinguished locals all had political or commercial backgrounds. Perhaps they might not have the impartiality that the job demanded.

It was up to Menzies, as Prime Minister, to make a recommendation to the Queen. He would probably do this on his February to Britain.

Letters, J James. We should have an English Governor General. It should be the means of cementing the relationship with the Mother Country, with whom we have everything in common.

A man with unbiased opinions would be a great inspiration to us all, as previous GGs have been, especially in the days of unrest and disquietude.

FEBRUARY: WHITE AUSTRALIA POLICY

Australia in 1961 persisted with its White Australia Policy (WAP). At the end of WWII, feelings against the Japanese were violent and people en masse swore they would never forgive them. Over the last 16 years, there had been some small revision of that attitude by the population in general, **though there were many who stood by their vow**. The other nations in Asia might or might not have fought against us, but in any case, the hostility felt to the Japanese inevitably spilled over to **all Asians**, so they too continued to be prohibited as migrants.

But travel to Asia was on the increase, the pain of War was diminishing with time, and business between us and them was growing. Some people were suggesting it was time we buried the hatchet, and allowed a quota to enter. A few people even went so far as to say we should put out the welcome mat **to the Japanese**.

Mr T Watkins of Camperdown wrote a substantial Letter which I have condensed down. He asked where would they be expected to work? Surely not in the north or the jungles. There is plenty of land in Asia that fits that description but they have not worked in those areas.

Does anyone believe that coloured people can be assimilated into a white community? He was able to point to many cases where they have not been. Would they be accepted by workers here? Not at all, because there would be the fear that they would undercut our wages and conditions. Our White Australia Policy was brought about by this very situation a century earlier.

Does anyone think the type of people we would accept would want to come? Certainly not, he says, we would just get the second-rate citizens. He concluded "I advocate the WAP be left as it is, as one of the few sensible moves made by any Australian Government, both in the interests of the Australian people and the coloured people themselves."

Letters, James Lyons. The main criticism of the WAP is that it is, in effect, **a racial policy** and not an economic one. The point is not whether coloured people would want to migrate to this country, but that our laws prevent them from doing so irrespective of their standard of education or other qualifications and purely on the basis of their race and colour. Many of us, not necessarily unworldly clergymen or unscrupulous businessmen, see a potential danger in the bad feelings created by such a policy of racial exclusiveness.

Difficulties in the assimilation of coloured migrants are usually due to the attitude of people who, like Mr Watkins, inevitably think of all non-Europeans as "coolies" belonging to inferior races.

Letters, Craster Usher. James Lyons and those who think like him not only live in a fools' paradise but would have us convert Australia into one. Short of a millennium in which all the races of the world embrace one religion, one set of marriage customs, traditions, etc., and become in fact one society, nations will have restrictive immigration policies based on race and the social customs of race.

Failing such a millennium, a multi-racial society or community can only exist if one particular racial group has political control. This is Britain's dilemma in central Africa and the dice are loaded against its plans for multi-racial societies there.

Quotas of Asian and African migrants presuppose that they and Australians are willing to intermarry without stigma on either side. The Christian religion has no monopoly of ethics, but although its views on the brotherhood of man may not, for example, be very different from those of Moslems, their respective marriage customs are vastly different.

Much of the talk about the "White Australia" policy stems from fear. But less talk and more action about our empty north would alleviate it. Over-populated Holland sends us many excellent migrants. Why not ask the Netherlands Government to help in a joint effort in which we should also fully exploit the inevitable exodus of Europeans from South and central Africa?

There remains the question of the Aborigines. They cannot be assimilated in the usually accepted sense of the word ("made like"). But, being few in number, they can be absorbed in the same way as the European race is absorbing the Maoris in New Zealand by generations of intermarriage.

FAMINE IN CHINA

One of the aims of the Cold War was to keep up a barrage of propaganda from a variety of sources, to convince people that one way of life was better than the other. So a common feature of the day was that someone would make a statement to the world, state a number of facts and a conclusion, and some one else would immediately dispute every utterance in the first statement.

China was the ideal place to pontificate on because it was far away, and in the hands of unfriendly rulers, so for most folk, it was hard to get verification of any facts. These Letters below demonstrate this, as well as the style of argument and controversy that got people excited in 1961.

Letters, Brian Buckley, President, Association for Human Rights, Kew, Victoria. In fact there has been a chronic famine in China at least since 1953 – the staple diet of the masses being sweet potatoes – while for the last 12 months it has been mounting to catastrophic proportions. This has been evident from the concentration of mainland medial journals on famine diseases, from letters of mainland Chinese to Hong Kong relatives, from refugees, and from revealing items in the Press.

The famine has been caused by the following basic factors: **First**, the economic planning of the regime, which concentrates on a power economy and neglects items essential to subsistence, such as the manufacture of chemical fertilizers. **Second**, the inadequacy of the Chinese railway system which is very poor and is now cluttered up with transport supporting the break-neck war program. **Thirdly,** the creation of the communes, and the consequent destruction of individual peasant incentive, in a country whose agriculture depends on irrigation, which requires for its success great personal care.

Yet since the Chinese Communists can afford to keep the starving masses down with a police apparatus of unprecedented savagery, it appears that they were prepared to take the death by starvation of millions in their stride as a price worth paying to turn China into a big military Power in the shortest possible time.

The deliberate extermination of millions, whether by hunger or the sword, is declared a crime under the United Nations Charter. Let us sell or give to the Chinese all the wheat they need, but let us not participate directly or indirectly in a propaganda fraud designed to hide from the world the extent of the crisis in the Communist quarter.

Letters, Leslie Haylen, MP. I have never heard of Brian Buckley's Association for Human Rights. The famine in China is not communist-inspired; neither is it induced by the industrial policy of Mao Tse-tung. It is a terrible agony to China that the sub-continent has been plagued by droughts and ravaged by floods from time immemorial. The overflowing of the great Chinese rivers in the past has claimed millions of lives a year. The day-by-day battle to feed the teeming millions of China breaks down when the droughts come and the rice dies.

Famine in China is as old as Chinese history. The only thing different today is that something is being done about it. The Chinese Government is scouring the world to supply wheat and other products for its hungry people. Australia has had a windfall by the sale of 27 million Pounds of wheat to China, and Canada is supplying even greater tonnage. China is spending its hard-won credits to feed her people; perhaps ruining, for the time being at least, her dream of becoming a great industrial Power. How Brian Buckley can see in this the deliberate extermination of a people is hard to understand.

The sad thing about this question is that some people can only see every situation through the eyes of hatred and prejudice. This is more deadly than any atom bomb.

Letters, Brian Buckley. If Mr Haylen were not a member of Parliament for the alternative Government party of this country, his insulting and confused letter could be ignored. Yet he is a public figure and we have to answer.

And answer he does. They continued to argue back and forth. One of these was a goodie, and the other was a baddie. I forget now which is which. These battles were everywhere and, very much like today, they never convinced anyone of anything.

PETROL VENDING MACHINES

News item. The NSW Labor Cabinet decided today not to allow petrol station owners to provide **petrol vending machines** for their customers. At the moment, these machines are forbidden in NSW, at any time of the day. The motion put forward was to allow them for after-hours service. All petrol stations must close in the very early evening, and for most of the week-end, and the fines for trading outside these times was yesterday doubled.

Cabinet took the view that there was ample time within trading hours to buy petrol, and that to go beyond them was unnecessary.

The argument raised yesterday was that **all** station owners could not afford the machines. This meant that those who could afford them would get more business that those who could not. This was not a fair competitive system. **No mention was made of the trade union opposition to the machines.**

Comment. What a joke. The service station owners and all of the employees saw that these machines might cut jobs. Thus they opposed their introduction. This was quite a sensible thing to do. But for the Cabinet to pretend that this was not an important issue, **and as a Labor Cabinet,** pretend it was not a factor in their decision,was fooling no one.

Letters, J Poole. The motorists of NSW, especially those living in the country, will want a better explanation from the State Labour Government why it persists in forbidding the use of automatic petrol dispensers outside of garage trading hours.

The Government seems to think that it does not have to give any reason why NSW motorists should be deprived of an after-hours petrol service that Victorian motorists have been enjoying for 12 months.

Whether the NSW Government likes it or not, the machine age is here to stay.

Letters, Thomas Esplin The State Government seems to be giving heed to the undoubted opposition to coin-operated petrol pumps instead of to the urgent need of many after-hours motorists.

The main objections are: **One**. The trade-unions, who fear the introduction of these pumps might put driveway attendants out of work.

Two. The service-station proprietors, objecting to the cost of the pumps, and unfair competition if they don't install them.

Three. The oil companies, complaining about the extra cost of delivery to more pumps and the loss to the after-hours petrol buyer of "driveway service" – cleaning the windscreen, checking water level in battery and radiator, checking oil level and tyre pressure, etc.

There is a way in which all these objections could be met, and it would ensure that the pumps were only used outside normal trading hours. If the pumps delivered, say, 1/9 worth of petrol for every 2/- inserted, the great majority of motorists would continue to obtain their petrol at the normal price during normal hours, and do away with the first objection.

Motorists urgently requiring after-hours petrol and unable to obtain it during normal hours would gladly pay the small surcharge for the new convenience. The extra threepence, split up twopence to the service-station owner and a penny to the oil company, should deal with the second and third objections. As for driveway service, the motorist can clean his own windscreen for once!

Nobody could claim he was penalized by the rise in price, as nobody would be forced to buy after hours – the choice would be his own. The Government might well give the scheme a trial.

OTHER VENDING MACHINES

Vending machines were in the news at the moment. An American company, International Vending Machines, had been making a big splash over the last two years selling a business proposition directly to the Oz population. Their spiel said a huge range of products, from cigarettes to chocolates to bottles of soft drink, were badly needed because we had virtually no shops open after 5.30pm, weekdays or most of the weekend. Anyone who wanted to exploit this could pay over a fairly large sum of money and buy a business. All they then had to do was keep up the supplies to the machine, collect the money, and keep an agreed proportion, and die rich. They were promised an annual return of around 25 per cent on their money, for an hour's work daily.

We poor gullible fools flocked to take advantage of this. And many people prospered for a couple of years. But as with all contrived schemes, when the flood of new money stopped coming in so fast, the payouts dried up, and investors were right now starting to rue the day. By March, the talk of bankruptcy was common, judges were warning too-late against entering into any such contracts, and operators were trying to off-load heaps of chocolates.

These however were not the only vending machines on the scene, as the writer below reminds us. He is concerned that he puts money into machines and expects to get stamps from them. But more often than not, the machine fails to deliver, His flippant note below conceals a real problem.

Letters, M Smith. Would it be possible for an inspector to be appointed to examine vending machines controlled by the Post Office?

Is the money contributed to the Post Office to be treated for income-tax purposes **as a donation to charity,** or an expense incurred in the vain hope of obtaining some gain? Is it possible to purchase shares in these vending machines, as I have always been a firm believer in a "money for nothing" business, providing I am on the receiving end instead of vice versa?

OUR NEXT GG: END OF MONTH NEWS

Mr Menzies had been Prime Minister for ten years, and he was quite comfortable in the job. One of the perks of office for him was to go overseas, normally to England, and elsewhere, once or twice a year. He liked the ceremony of London and the ability to strut his stuff among world leaders. He revelled in his own oratory, and was pleased when people compared him, as they always did, to the war-time Churchill. He very much enjoyed his visits to the Queen, and even at one stage had regaled her with lines of poetry he had written about her.

One of his tasks in London this year was to have the Queen make the right selection for the position of Governor General. The time-honoured system was that he would put three suggestions to the Queen, who would then discuss them with Menzies and the high and mighty, and then appoint the most suitable person. All of this was very hush-hush, and no one outside a small circle knew any details. This of course prompted the journalists of that fair city to speculate wildly on who the lucky winner would be.

Now, true to form, they came up with two highly-favoured candidates. First, was the retiring Chief of General Staff, Field Marshall Festing. "He is aged 58, likes the outdoor life, and was delighted with Australia on his two previous visits." According to rumour, he had been strongly fancied for the position for a long time.

"The dark horse is a man twenty years younger. The Earl of Harewood is an ex-prisoner of war, and is a patron of the Arts. Soon after the War he caused a stir by marrying a commoner, a beautiful Austrian girl, who comes from a famous musical family, and who is a distinguished pianist herself. The Earl is an artistic director of the Edinburgh Festival, and has one of the finest of art collections in Britain."

Back home, the Federal Opposition were still going on about appointing an Australian. There was **not the slightest chance that Menzies would do that**, but it seemed that there might be a few votes in complaining about the situation.

They were boosted in their efforts by a Gallup Poll that showed that 63 per cent wanted an Australian, 13 per cent a member of the Royal family, and 18 per cent wanted some other Englishman. But this was one thing that Menzies never showed any signs of listening to. **I will bet you**

that there is some very blue blood coming our way soon after Menzies gets back.

HOLD THAT TIGER

Prince Phillip, and his good wife, Queen Elizabeth of England, popped off to India for a tour of that Dominion. Reports soon came through that the Duke had bagged an 8-foot tiger on his third expedition. He had been placed on a 25ft high platform when the 200 beaters forced the tiger into the clearing below. The Duke fired and the beast went down at the first shot. The Queen watched from another platform about 30 yards away, and captured the exciting moment on film.

The Queen and Duke were spending two days relaxing at the hunting lodge as guests of the Maharajah. They left by train that night to resume their tour of India.

Comment. The concern of the world about animal welfare was nowhere to be seen. Lobby groups had not yet formed, and protests came from individuals who had not yet **amalgamated into groups.**

MARCH: NEWS FROM SOUTH AFRICA

In the last few years, the black majority in South Africa had been getting more active, and sometimes violent, in their quest for greater freedoms. The white community, remembering that they had developed the land over a century and more, were intent on holding on to the power and wealth they had accumulated, while the blacks wanted all the freedoms and equalities that they knew were possible. Last year, the world was startled by riots at Sharpville that cost many lives, and by the non-fatal shooting of the Prime Minister, Mr Verwoerd.

The British Empire had given way to a more liberal arrangement of nations called the British Commonwealth, and most years held a Meeting of representatives from each of the 12 participating nations. The white nations were Australia, Britain, Canada, New Zealand. And South Africa. The coloured nations included India, Malaya, and Singapore, and ex-colonies from Africa.

Every one of these nations had concerns that **its** internal affairs might be talked about at the Meeting, so they were **each careful not to discuss the internal affairs of any other member** there. After all, so the reasoning went, Australia can be doing, or not doing, dreadful things to her natives, but **that is an internal matter, and we expect that no one will raise it.**

SOUTH AFRICA IN 1961

This year the Meeting was due to be held in London in March, but before that, in an unprecedented move, a number of the black nations, and Canada, spoke vehemently against South Africa. Nigeria described SA's conduct as a gross violation of human rights, Malaya's Tunku Abdul Rahman said it was an offence against humanity, and Cyprus asked the inevitable question of whether SA could be firmly criticised and still stay in the Commonwealth. No one before had been subjected to such devastating attacks, and it was not clear if a way could be found that **abhorred the policy of Apartheid** but **accepted the nation**.

Over the first few days of the meeting, SA and the white nations muddled round, and then, when they were on the verge of finding a compromise, the SA Prime Minister, Dr Verwoerd, **announced that his Government had decided to leave the Commonwealth.** He said that the Prime Ministers had shown a degree of animosity, and had launched unbridled attacks on South Africa. He singled out the Asian nations and Canada for blame, and made it clear that there was no hope of South Africa returning to the fold.

The other countries were quite apprehensive. This bloc of nations was the third most powerful in the world. If they hung together, they could have some measure of influence over the two super-powers, Russia and America, but if they each went their own merry way, they were almost powerless. Yet here they were potentially starting the process of disintegration. South Africa had gone. Did they know who might be next? They had broken the custom of not speaking about each other's faults and weaknesses, could any one of them say that it was not vulnerable in the same way?

For Australia, **our first weakness** obviously lay in our treatment of the Aborigines. They were treated differently, and treated poorly, and there was no vestige of equality for them in our society. **The second weakness** was our White Australia Policy, where people were excluded because of their Asian race. It was true that the South African natives were actually meeting physical violence in large quantities, so you could agree that their plight was worse than anything we were causing. **On the other hand**, you could argue that a gross injustice is just that, and the difference was only a matter of degree, and perhaps just a matter of time. In any case, as a nation we were not above reproach, and many of our politicians spent time looking over their shoulders in international courts.

Letters, Bill Arthur. Mr Arthur Calwell, Leader of the Federal Opposition, should be the last person to assert that the Prime Minister, Mr Menzies, is likely to give Australia a bad name in Asia. Mr Calwell's handling of his portfolio when he was Minister for Immigration did more harm to Australia's reputation in Asia than any other collection of Ministers this century. In the Philippines, people still talk bitterly about the treatment meted out to Sergeant Gamboa by Mr Calwell and the Labour Government. And all Asians remember Mrs O'Keefe.

On a recent journey through Asia I found that our Prime Minister was held in very high regard by Asian people, and that Australia's reputation, as a result of the Colombo Plan, was very high. The worst thing that could happen to Australia's reputation in Asia would be for Mr Calwell to become Prime Minister.

Comment. The prestige of the nation depended largely on those very few people from here who made the news overseas. The Leader of the Opposition had for years taken supposedly populist stances on issues, gambling that the average Aussie would rally to him if he put the boot into Asians. But his reputation overseas was very dubious when compared to the careful Menzies.

The situation in South Africa slowly developed. We will come back to it.

KIDNAPPER GUILTY

On March 30th Stephen Leslie Bradley was found guilty of the 1960 murder of schoolboy Graeme Thorne, and was sentenced to life imprisonment. He claimed innocence of the crime, though no person who listened to the police case could believe that for a moment. He would probably, with good behaviour, serve 12 to 14 years.

Hundreds of people, mainly women, filled the courtroom, and many of them sobbed and collapsed and showed other signs of relief when the verdict was announced. One woman screamed "Feed him to the sharks."

Bradley had kidnapped the boy to gain a ransom. He put him in the boot of his car and virtually kept him there till his death. He was arrested fleeing to England, and brought back to Australia. The Court case was the end of a drama that had stirred the nation. When it all happened, no one could believe that this type of crime could come to

Australia. It was the end of an age of innocence for every person in the community.

MIGRANT WOMEN IN THE WORKFORCE

Letters, A Fatseas.   Much irrationality and lack of adequate information were evident in F Micallef's letter complaining of employers' reluctance to employ migrant women who cannot speak English. While many thousands of such women are in fact employed in factories and other places, his criticism of employers who are disinclined to have such a staff is indeed absurd.

Why should an employer have to put up with all the onerous difficulties involved in trying to communicate with the foreign-tongued, plus an inefficient service resulting usually from the employee's inability to converse in the language spoken at her place of employment?

These women alone can solve their problem by making an honest effort to learn English instead of adopting an indifferent attitude and considering the language as something only their menfolk require. Even though this is not the general rule, the percentage of those apathetic to the learning of English is so high that it would only take the fulfilment of Mr Micallef's wish to convince these women, indeed all migrants, that English in Australia is now unnecessary.

That English is a language not easily learnt by an adult, is conceded. But no language in the world could be learnt by anyone who, with the thought of returning home in his mind, sees no urgent reason to burden himself with knowledge of temporary use.

PIN-BALL MENACE TO SOCIETY

Letters, D Downs. In recent months a "pin-ball machine" disease has spread through Sydney and suburbs, and is now reaching epidemic proportions. Milk bars and hamburger shops have installed them in large numbers, so that their clientele of juvenile delinquents can happily fritter away their wages. Perhaps we can condone the attitude of the milk bar and hamburger proprietors in the same manner as we condone poker machines in licensed clubs.

But surely the line must be drawn somewhere. Today I walked into a corner grocery shop and spied a newly installed neon-lit-sixpence-eater. Clustered around it was a group of six boys, aged from 10 to 14 years, busily pouring their pocket-money into the never satisfied slot.

Can these machines not be kept out of reach of children? Does the community really need a training ground for future poker machine addicts?

THE OPERA HOUSE OPENING

Letters, John Dudley. The building of our Opera House is quickly nearing the stage when the opening season should be arranged. May I suggest that our own Joan Sutherland, who has brought more to the operatic stage than any other singer since Melba, should be given the honour of appearing on this occasion in any one of her outstanding roles?

PAY YOUR LISTENERS' FEES

Letters, K Wyatt. The PMG Department needs to change its methods of catching "criminals" who fail to renew annual radio and TV licences.

Last year we got all in a bother because we couldn't find either. We vowed not to be caught red-faced again. Thus, we produced the required document. But it turned out to be an overdue notice – unpaid.

Well, had we or hadn't we? Could the inspector check his records? Not on your life he couldn't. The licence is supposed to be produced on demand, didn't we know. He then required us to switch on the TV, switch on the radio and noted the channel station to which we were tuned.

What was this, we asked. If we promised never to listen to the ABC again, could we go licence-free? No indeed. He said: We do this so we can say you were actually using the sets if we decide to prosecute.

But surely the law does not require a man to incriminate himself. Surely the Department could be content to require careless, can't-find, people to produce their licence within a specified time – or else.

Comment. The cost of these inspectors was big. The Post Masters General's Department was asked many times to produce evidence that the inspectors served some useful purpose. But this was never done. The entire population thought, probably correctly, that it was all just a revenue-raising stunt to keep the inspectors in a job.

Letters, R Stewart, Coogee. Surely it is time that the "ballyhoo" about drip-dry shirts was debunked. After the first wash they are shabby and compare most unfavourably with a good cotton shirt ironed in the usual way. Being a bachelor, I stocked up with drip-dry shirts and find them unsatisfactory. The process mentioned above spoils them for ironing.

LEG WARMERS

Letters, A Smith, Lane Cove. We are assailed on every side by the plea to use more wool and because my small schoolgirl daughters were complaining bitterly about the coldness of their leg (which were encased in nylon stockings) I remembered those warm ribbed stockings which kept the schoolgirls of my day so snug. No matter how biting the wind we were warm and the fact of ownership gave one a grown-up glamour.

Need I say I am still looking for them. I have been told by the largest and the smallest stores: "Everything is nylon or wool-nylon now, madam." The fact that I want to buy woollen stockings is tantamount to the rankest heresy, but on behalf of that vast army of small girls cannot some manufacturer help to o feel the blissful warmth of a pair of woollen stockings?

BUY AUSTRALIAN

Marketing bodies in Australia had decided that people here were buying too many overseas goods. One solution, for them, would be to restrict imports. But this would have gone against everything that we were currently working towards. We were, in fact, dismantling our trade barriers and slowly moving to the American ideal of free trade. There was little chance of restrictions or increased tariffs landing on non-essential goods.

The solution appeared to be to encourage locals to buy more Australian goods. To do this, the Chamber of Manufacturers launched a huge advertising campaign, urging the purchase of Oz goods. Not everyone thought that this was a good idea.

Letters, Mary Field. If the hideous full-page advertisement of the Chamber hopes to persuade me to buy Australian goods, it is very much mistaken. I buy for value for the money I spend; I like to get my money's worth – and, indeed, who doesn't? They seem to be asking us to buy Australian goods simply because they're Australian. Nobody is going to be that servile.

I don't think Australian goods are, in the main, inferior. They go all over the world; their reputation is high. A small example – when I was in London I was told repeatedly that Australian tinned jams were much more popular than most local brands.

Surely the whole point of this advertising should be that Australian goods are not inferior; that they give you your money's worth; that a false picture of the supposed glamour and quality of "imported' goods has been so drilled into us that the well-known Australian characteristic of inferiority has been artificially encouraged.

Finally, the advertisement is so horrible visually, its design is so appalling, that this must automatically rub off on to the goods it is trying to sell. It implies that the goods are as badly designed as the advertisement that is trying to sell them. We women, who decide most purchases, are not nearly so blind and bewildered as the Associated Chambers of Manufactures seem to think.

APRIL: WHO'S FAVOURITE FOR GG?

The rumour mongers are still going full bore on who the next GG will be.

Press report. Sources close to the Palace in London have announced that there are two outstanding persons who could are being considered for Governor General of Australia. The first is Lord de L'Isle, aged 52, a former Secretary for Air, and Managing Director of Schweppes in Britain. The second is Lord Cobbold, 57, and he is the retiring Governor of the Bank of England. It is understood that these two gentlemen were on the list of nominees tendered recently by the Australian Prime Minister, Mr Menzies, to the Queen. A rumour is circulating that Lord de L'Isle has been offered the post, but Buckingham Palace officials refused to comment.

Lord de L'Isle won the Victoria Cross in February, 1944, while serving as Major William Sydney with the Grenadier Guards at the Anzio beachhead. He is a descendant of the famous Elizabethan poet and soldier, Sir Philip Sydney. Observers believe he may have been recommended to Mr Menzies by Sir Winston Churchill. There is some speculation that he might refuse the post because of his business ambitions.

Lord Cobbold will retire in June after 11 years as Governor of the Bank of England. However, his wife had said that after retirement he will undertake no public work for six months.

"It seems certain that Australia will not be prepared to wait until 1962 without a Governor-General, however well-equipped Lord Cobbold may be for the task," says the *Sunday Telegraph* columnist. Lord Cobbold was not available for comment.

Comment. The newspapers were getting very excited about who might get the job. Probably, the persons in the above article **had** actually been on the list that the Queen discussed, and so each must have had a semblance of a chance.

The Oz populace was a bit ambivalent about it all. We were still very much interested in the Royal Family, our loyalty to the Crown and the Commonwealth was as yet untested by talk of a republic, and a visit to England was always on the itinerary of our young folk. All of this despite the steady stream of European migrants who were reducing the concentration of British stock in the population.

So everyone was interested in who the GG would be, and yet only a tiny minority saw him as having any useful role to play in Australia, and most people saw him as an odd throw-back to the glory days of Britain. He was good for ceremonies and church fetes, and if they got to meet him and shake hands, that would be great to talk about. But if a new bloke had not turned up for the job, very very few would have cared.

ROLL UP, ROLL UP ....

The Royal Easter Show was on again at Easter in Sydney. This was always billed of course as "The Greatest Show on Earth", and indeed it was spectacular. It ran for about two weeks, and covered just about every aspect of agriculture and animal-ware you could think of. Once again, in 1961, it attracted record attendances, and was rated a huge success.

However, while it was open on Good Friday, there was virtually no public transport and what was available started late, and stopped in the mid-afternoon. Attendances were down compared to other days, there were fewer ring events, and some of the side-shows did not open. So, it was a pretty drab day. Two hapless Letter-writers, doubtless bored witless, decided that they should complain about things shutting down on various days, and wrote simple little whinging notes to the *SMH*. The responses were more than they bargained for.

Letters, A Fagan. Is our Australia a free country or are we regimented by a minority group? On Good Friday and Sundays, sports, films, hotels and dances are forbidden by order of a dictating minority of senior women and sectarian ministers.

This minority abominated 10 o'clock closing. Several years of civilised hotel entertainment have proved them wrong. A few weeks' trial would prove even more the moral, social and cultural benefits of civilised holidays.

Letters, B H Dalton, Greenwich Point. After a grimly gloomy Good Friday, I ask: Is it really necessary to shut the taverns, and is the absence of newspapers, after many years, due to piety or to parsimony?

Letters, E C Savage, Windang. May I express my satisfaction at the news that the attendance at the Royal Easter Show on Good Friday was not as great as that of last year?

I do not criticise the Show, as a show. It is magnificent, and deserving of every praise and success; but the continued decision of the Committee to violate the distinctive nature of Good Friday moves me to hope that the Friday attendances will continue to fall to a point where it will be disastrous to continue.

Whether the Committee likes it or not, Australia is accepted as a Christian nation. Our laws, customs and observances are based upon the Christian ethic. That should be enough for the official voice of the country at least to proclaim, and in the I include such a thing as the Show, which purports to demonstrate Australia to the world.

It matters not that there may be Jews, Moslems, agnostics of every kind, even atheists, among us – in the eyes of the world we are classed as a Christian nation. Therefore, either the Committee should disavow its Christianity, or close the Show on the day of the year which is peculiarly Christian. Government circles should disavow either the Show, or their Christianity too, on Good Friday; the Police Force, for instance did not have to allow its members to participate in the events in which they did take part.

The time for protest is not next year, when the members of the Committee will again be able to hide behind a *fait accompli,* but **now** while these presumably Christian gentlemen are still reckoning the value of the takings for this Good Friday, and presumably, concluding that their belief does not pay them half so well.

Letters, R Wallace. With regard to the opening of the Royal Show on Good Friday – a holiday, or, more correctly, a Holy Day commemorating the Crucifixion, which all other entertainments respect by remaining closed – the general opinion seems to be that the Show is classed as an "educational" exhibition and not as an entertainment. Whether the sideshows, ring competitions, woodchopping, etc., can be classed as "educational" may be left to more competent authorities.

The reason usually given for opening the Show on Good Friday is that the Show would lose heavily by closing on that day. As an alternative, and so that the Show may not suffer financially, may I suggest that in place of Good Friday, the Show be allowed to open on Easter Sunday. The idea will of course shock earnest Christians, but since "the Show must go on" it is perhaps preferable that it should be held on the day commemorating the Resurrection, rather than on the day of the Crucifixion.

Letters, J Fisher. Does it occur to the people objecting to a "gloomy" Good Friday that the only reason for observing the day at all is its religious significance?

If they don't wish to observe it as the most solemn day in the Christian year, why take a holiday at all? Why not just treat it as an ordinary working day? They can't have it both ways.

Letters, C Cameron. A Fagan deplores our so-called "gloomy" Good Friday. He mentions moral, social and cultural benefits in his criticism, but omits spiritual benefits. Should he not have signed himself "A Pagan" instead of A Fagan?

Letters, A Levenson. On Good Friday, a turn of the dial to any radio station brought a veritable feast of good music, and even the commercial announcements were tolerable. Alas, it was only a temporary respite from the inane noises that pass for music.

My point in writing – why only on Good Friday?

THE BAY OF PIGS

Back in 1958, Fidel Castro led a successful and popular uprising against the Government of Cuba, and was able to establish a regime, which he headed, that was very strongly nationalistic. Over the last two years, he had introduced a number of measures that had taken away a great deal of land and wealth and power from large American companies, and at the same time he had started to talk to the Russian Premier, Nikita Khruschev, and to tinker with the notion of Cuba's becoming a Communist state.

None of these latter measures pleased the American hierarchy, including the CIA, and for months the rumours had been circulating that America was about to invade Cuba. In mid April, a number of desultory raids were carried out on a few ports and airfields, and then on April 18th an armed force of 1,500 Cuban expats invaded the Island.

The situation was very confused for days, because this was not an official invasion, and thus the State Department was at pains to distance itself from it. It turned out that the CIA had trained the invaders, and equipped them, and landed them ashore in the expectation that the population would rise up and expel Castro. Nothing of the sort happened, and within three days, Castro was able to claim total victory.

The US was very embarrassed. It became obvious quickly that the CIA had been behind the plot, and therefore the buck stopped with President Kennedy. Despite having been kept in the dark about the operation, he did take responsibility and thus made the fiasco a much-publicised Government failure. In the Cold War world, such a blunder was seen to be of considerable importance, and one that haunted international relations for years.

This *SMH* Editorial summed up the frustration of the Western world at the incompetence.

"As a result the American dilemma is now more difficult than ever. Dr Castro's prestige must be greatly strengthened. He now has his excuse to strengthen his ties with Russia still further and to enlarge his police state measures. The forces of Castroism must be strengthened throughout the hemisphere.

The West has suffered yet another defeat, this time in a battle, important to its interests, in which it could neither fight itself nor greatly help those fighting for it. The incident glaringly illuminates the contrast between Russia's ability and western inability to advance its cause through the problems and convulsions of our revolutionary world."

YURI GAGARAN SPACED OUT

What made matters worse for the America was that a week earlier, **Russia had put the first man into outer space.** For the last two years, a veritable traffic jam of dogs, mice, monkeys, and sea urchins had filled space, and seemingly made it so crowded that any man would be wise to stay on earth. But not daunted, the Russians on April 12 fired a man into space, and brought him safely back to earth one hour and 48 minutes later. During that time, Yuri Gagarin made one orbit of the earth in his four-ton spaceship, in "the greatest achievement in the history of man", according to many Western scientists.

Russia, and the Communist world, was ecstatic. President Kennedy and the British Prime Minister sent hearty congratulations. Some American Pentagon sources immediately saw the feat as a threat to the US, and responded with sour grapes. Indeed a few of our own dignitaries were remarkably off-hand, or even rude, but most of the world was genuinely impressed. Apart from being a major conquest for science, **it was an enormous Cold War propaganda victory for the Russians, and they were quite prepared to dwell on it at length**.

World Press coverage was generous. But particularly so in Russia, There, it was reported, scenes bordering on mass hysteria welcomed Gagaren on his return. The crowds went wild with delight during the airport welcome, the drive to the city and the rally in Red Square.

In one of the most emotional scenes, the Soviet Premier, Mr Khrushcvhev, almost in tears, embraced Major Gagaran and kissed him repeatedly on the mouth and cheeks.

Throughout the day, 20-gun salutes boomed out in Moscow and other Soviet cities in honour of the Major. He had been greeted earlier by a cheering crowd at Moscow airport as he stepped from the airliner. Saluting Mr Khrushchev, he made a 30-second speech.

Mr Khrushchev threw formality overboard and kissed Gagaran, again full on the mouth. Other Soviet leaders, caught up in the emotional atmosphere, kissed Major Gagaran in turn. Only the playing of the National anthem brought them back to reality, but did not stop the crowd from shouting and cheering.

As the martial strains rang out, they pushed and struggled to get a closer look at a space hero. Then the anthem was over, and the emotion on the official platform broke out anew.

The Letters pages of the *SMH* celebrated the flight with a **curious** discussion on just how brave Gagarin was. You can glean from these that **there were more sour grapes in Oz than in most parts of the globe**. As was often the case in those days, a good deal of religious thought got into the debate.

> **Letters, (Rev) D Rose.** Mr Khrushchev says that the first cosmonaut's "courage, gallantry and heroism in the name of service to mankind" will be remembered down the centuries.
>
> Although the scientific feat is unmatched in history, can we agree that the courage of the passenger is an outstanding example to mankind? Has it not been matched and exceeded in every century and even in every year? Is it greater than

that of the lifesaver who propels himself far from land with only his skin between him and shark-infested water?

In the history of new explorations, we have countless examples of men who braved more than the possibility of some moments of extreme pain. They braved the certainty of severe hardships to be endured over weeks and months as well as repeated risk of their lives.

When Major Gagarin sat cushioned in his air-conditioned compartment ,he knew that his chances of unscathed survival had been demonstrated by canine predecessors. He also knew that his rigours would be followed in minutes by the best of medical attention.

He may be the hero of the week amid the Moscow cries of "Glory be to the first Soviet Cosmonaut," but when it comes to the heroism of centuries he has not for a moment outshone the memory of those persecuted Christians of so many years ago who suffered and died and asked no glory but the glory of God.

Letters, Miriam Hampson. As one of the public who feels that April 12, 1961, marked a great event in the advancement of mankind, I would like to say all honour to the Soviet scientists for their great achievement. I feel sure I am not alone in finding the remarks of our scientists, **Sir Norman Eccles with his "little value," and Professor Oliphant's "a stunt," very hard to understand.**

It is strange to find the scientists of this country has helped considerably to "blaze a trail to the stars" with our great aviators such as Bert Hinkler, Sir Charles Kingsford Smith, Charles Ulm and others, **adopting such an ungenerous attitude**.

Letters, Alex Carey, Kirrawee. The Rev Rose questions whether the courage of the Russian spaceman can be reckoned at all comparable with the heroism of Christian martyrs of long ago.

Such a question raises some nice problems, for one must take into account that Major Gagarin, presumably, does not believe in a life after death. Does it, then, require more courage to risk death in the modest discomfort of a spaceship when one believes death to involve final annihilation? Or, to face certain death via the exceeding discomfort of a lion's jaws when one believes death but a prelude to life everlasting and eternal joy?

Personally I find the second a more fearsome and exacting alternative. But perhaps that is because I have never been able to muster a very vivid confidence in a life hereafter for me personally. I would be very interested to know what a Christian of real faith would make of these alternatives.

Letters, J Abbott. Sir John Eccles' view is not "ungenerous". He means that society, through its Governments, is being disproportionately, lavishly, indeed quite wickedly, "generous" to one field of human endeavour, while vast areas of research and of human need stagger along in their old, age-long penury. Sir John Eccles, and just a few people of vision here and there, perceive the tragic imbalance.

Letters, John F Cole. The Rev Rose does not seem to realise the true magnitude of the feat accomplished by Russia, or the courage of Major Gagarin.

I believe that this event is as significant in our time as was the first manned balloon or aeroplane flight of years gone by. Are not then, the Russians justified in setting up Gagarin as a State hero? The unconcerned attitude of most people outside scientific and political circles would appear to deny the intrinsic magnitude of the feat.

I venture to say that a lifesaver's courage amounts to very little when compared with the courage of Gagarin and I wonder how many lifesavers would have taken his place if it had been offered them? The Christian martyrs' great courage until death was not their own, but rather a manifestation of the power of Christ within them; even so, they gained a great deal by death. Major Gagarin had nothing to gain by death, nor did he have any power but his own to enable him to carry out his task.

Letters, R G W. J Abbott writes that "Sir John Eccles and just a few people of vision here and there perceive the tragic imbalance."

Dr J H Coles, delivering his Mulvey Oration on March 20 at a medical gathering in Goulburn of the Federation of Country Local Associations, stated: "The glamour of putting a man into space seems far more important than the millions of reasons for keeping him healthy on earth, and the thousands of better reasons for attempting to prevent the necessity of putting him under the earth prematurely."

Quote from the Archbishop of Canterbury. "The only people impressed by this space business are those who have nothing better to think of, poor fellows."

AT LAST: MENZIES COMES CLEAN

On April 11th, the Queen and Mr Menzies jointly announced that Lord de L'Isle was to be our next GG. This gentleman was seen as perfect for the role, and Mr Menzies expressed his delight that he had accepted the post, and thought he would take up the position in a month or two.

Lord De L'Isle **was married** and had five children, four of whom would accompany their parents to Australia. No arrangements had yet been made for their schooling. Until now, they had never attended school, but had been instructed by governesses and tutors.

All three children had something of a title. For example, the married daughter was The Right Honourable Elizabeth, while the son was the Right Honorable Philip.

MAYBE WE SHOULD PRAY A BIT

Not everyone was apathetic about the war threats. This lady suggests there is another way out of the situation.

Letters. Anne Mack, Bondi. With war and annihilation threatening the world, I have been surprised that not one of the religious leaders have suggested calling the nation to prayer. I am not a regular church-goer, but I have a very strong belief in prayer.

Comment. I too was surprised. Granted we in Oz were not so worked up about it all. But that had not stopped people in the past calling for prayers to stop wars, end the droughts, kill the rabbits, and keep Melbourne dry for the 1956 Olympics.

During WWII such calls were non-stop. For the next 15 years, they appeared every time we had a problem of enough magnitude. However in the last 5 years or so, they almost disappeared. This coincided with the obvious secularisation of society, and with the increasing drift away from the churches and organised religions.

LIVING CHESS IS NOT NEW

Letters, F Dawson I read where a game of living chess is to be played for the first time in Australia. I would like to say that one of my happiest childhood memories is that I took part (pawn red) in a living chess game during the Tasmanian International Exhibition (1892-4).

NO PHONE BILLS

Letters, D Yates, Coogee. I think the introduction of coin-operated telephones for domestic use would be a good idea. How many subscribers are faced with large accounts which have been boosted by the free use of their telephone by guests, callers, neighbours, etc? Many such calls are due to a sense of hospitality to guests and many by droppers-in who unwittingly, or otherwise, neglect to pay for their calls.

A money-box shrewdly place by the telephone is distasteful to me and I must be frank – I would hate to accept payments from guests for calls. The present credit system of telephone accounts, therefore, produces social and financial discomfort.

The mandatory insertion of a coin for private calls would mean that everyone would pay for their own calls and the subscriber would have no bills to pay.

HAPPY ENDINGS

Letters, B Fielder, Forestville. Last night a heated argument wore 10 of us to the point of exhaustion.

In making up our fourth party for "My Fair Lady", a discussion arose as to why it lured us yet again. Although we all agreed with the three intellectuals of our party that it was stimulating, scintillating, intellectual, rich in acting opportunity and wonderful theatre, the seven non-intellectuals maintained that its real attraction lay in its beauty of presentation and its romance.

Why can't we have more plays that are lovely and romantic, so that we may relax in our seats and allow sweet illusion to waft about us? The crowds who are sick of gutter plays will not only come – they will leave the theatre smiling and with a little tender glow in their hearts.

LUCKY PARENTS OF QUADS

Letters, J Hardy. I find it ludicrous that a family, Australian or otherwise, should be given presents of considerable value because the wife gave birth to quadruplets, something over which she had no control. Why these people should be singled out for such a windfall because they are the parents of four children is something beyond my comprehension. Surely there are enough widows with children, pensioners, orphans, etc., who would be better benefited by such gifts – now they have to struggle along the best they can.

COMIC HEROES ARE GONE

Since WWII, Australian children, followed by their parents had raced to the Sunday Papers to get hold of the Comic Section. There they could find heroes like Superman, Dick Tracy, Joe Palooka, the Saint, the Phantom, and Prince Valient..

There were many other quaint but interesting characters. For example, Nancy, Ginger Meggs, Dagwood, Bib and Bub, the Katzenjama Twins, and Little Abner.

Alas, by 1970, there are mainly gone from Australia.
They are badly missed.

MAY: OZ GOVERNMENT BEWARE

The Oz economy was going along reasonably well, but there were some signs that things were quietly deteriorating. Everyone knew that the credit squeeze was curtailing business, and that the heat had been taken out of the economy. The Treasurer, Holt, had recently said that there would be no further relaxation of the restrictive controls until next June, at the earliest. But the question that was gnawing away was whether the economy was slowing down **too** much. Had the brakes been applied too hard, and would there be a sudden recession? Despite the Government's non-stop whistling in the dark, a number of things suggested that this might be the case.

For example, BHP had just laid off 850 men. The Hire Purchase industry reported that outstandings were noticeably down on last year. The wool industry, that Oz was still riding on, also reported deteriorating sales. No particular indicator alone was convincing, but together they were a cause for concern. Yet against those, there was plenty of work available, though there was a "**drift** rather than a **fall** in employment". People were able to pay off their mortgages and hire purchase debt, and an increasing number were sending their kids to private schools.

So, the situation was up in the air. No one could claim that things were really good, nor could anyone claim we were on the brink. But, the advice to the nation could well have been: ***Proceed with Caution.***

IN WEST NEW GUINEA: CAUTION

Caution was needed with the Indonesians in their claim for West New Guinea. Since World War II, nationalists in Indonesia had been working hard to bring their scattered islands under one government, and to establish all the systems needed for this. By 1961, this very difficult task was nearing completion, and West New Guinea was one of the few remaining lands that was still outstanding.

The Dutch, however, still occupied that land, and were claiming that it should continue to live under her flag. General Nasution, the Indonesian Foreign Minister, had just spent a week in Australia talking to Menzies and Foreign Affairs and the like, and had been told that, while we were looking for a peaceful solution to the Indonesian claim, **we recognised the Dutch** as being the correct custodian of the land.

When he returned home, he made a statement to the effect that he had been well received in Australia, and his visit had confirmed that Australia had no treaty with the Dutch, but that **it did still recognise Dutch sovereignty towards West Irian** (Dutch New Guinea). He pointed out that Australia hoped that the two parties involved would work out a solution between themselves, and that Australia did not see us getting involved. Though in answer to a question, he did add that "if an incident did occur that involved the Dutch, it may lead to open war. What Australia's stand would then be would depend on the situation. But, if such an event happened, there would be a **liquidation of all Dutch assets in Indonesia**."

There was nothing immediately worrying there. But the fact that we still recognised the Dutch as the rightful rulers got many parties and newspapers in Indonesia very agitated. For example, the pressure group *1945 Generation* said that Menzies' stance would arouse the people's anger. "It is now obvious that Australia not only misunderstands our claims, but **it is also making itself the enemy of the Indonesian people** who are struggling for the recovery of West Irian. They are still defending colonialism, and they vindicate the atrocities in that land. There is no power in the world that can stem the current surge for freedom in Asia, and prevent the removal of our colonial shackles."

Comment. That type of non-official talk was worrying. Often, such talk was a second-level way of getting a here's-what-we-**really**-think message through to outsiders. So, it would seem that at this point, once again the Oz government should *Proceed with Caution*, and avoid nasty complications with our nearest northern neighbours.

QUESTIONS OF COLOUR

The world was becoming colour conscious. All of Africa was in the process of throwing out the white man, or reducing his wealth and power. In Asia, in countries such as Indonesia, nationalism and anti-imperialism were rampant.

In America, blacks were fighting for some semblance of equality with the whites, and were copping a hiding as a result. Every day our papers were reporting on riots, and police brutality, whippings of blacks, **and** whippings of white people who sympathised with the blacks. Troops were everywhere pushing people off university campuses, and harassing them with tear gas and drawn bayonets and sometimes shooting them. Freedom Rides were banned, or disrupted, or proscribed.

Against this background, events in Australia were small beer. Nevertheless, on a number of fronts, things were happening, as is shown by the mixture of reports below. The first Letter is quite long, but it expresses many points that were raised by other writers in half a dozen Letters.

Letters, Mona Brand. For the past few days we have had staying with us a visitor from another planet – from Mars, to be exact. He came to earth to study our laws and social customs.

The other day he came to me and said: "Yesterday in a Sydney suburb I met a Mr Brown. In talking to him I discovered that he often borrows money from young people, has not been working regularly, and owes his landlord rent. Do you think we should report him to the authorities?"

"Whatever for?" I asked. "In order," said the Martian, "to have taken from him his right to vote, to drink in the hotel with his friends, and all his other rights as an Australian citizen." "That is not the law!" I retorted hotly. "Pardon me," said the other, "but I believe it is. Here is a case of this very thing described in your 'Sydney Morning Herald' of May 17," and he drew a cutting from his pocket.

"Ah," I said after I had read the item, "this Mr Brown of yours – what colour is his skin?" "White," said the Martian, "does that make all the difference?"

"Not all of it. Tell me – when did his forbears come to Australia?" "Two generations ago. What has that to do with it?" "Everything," I said. "You see, the Mr Mulberry referred to in this newspaper item is a descendant of the original inhabitants of this country. His people have been here, in our land, Australia for thousands of years."

"And this is a reason for his being denied Australian citizenship as his birthright, although his shortcomings are no worse than those of the white man whose family came here from across the ocean in comparatively recent times?"

"Certainly!"

"But why?"

"Why?" I echoed, "for his own protection, of course".

I thought this incident might be of some interest to your readers.

Comment. Right now, in 1961, we were **at the start** of a decade that saw "coloured" people all over the world gain some of the rights and privileges that were taken for granted by the "whites". When I look back to a decade earlier, there were only a few intrepid campaigners writing Letters such as the one above, and their voices were in the wilderness.

Now, especially given the ferment overseas, the rights of Aborigines were being discussed and considered in more and more quarters. At the moment, such discussion tended to be on **one matter at a time.** It might be voting rights, or it might be alcohol laws and their application, it might be access to public swimming pools. Rarely, however, at this stage, did it move to more abstract topics such as the dignity of the Aborigines, and their unconstrained right to be considered as equals in all matters. Not just under the law, but also throughout every aspect of their lives as they lived them.

Now, however, we were indeed at **the start** of the process. Over the last 50 years, we have seen much progress, with hopefully more to come. We have a long way to go.

Comment two. We will see some talk of **assimilation**. Very popular about this time in the United States, this meant that all people should be thrown into the melting pot, and we would all come out the colour of weak tea, and with philosophies and cultures to match. At the **other extreme** were the advocates of letting races and nationalities settle in **"ghettos"**, and thereby keep their language, and customs, and culture all to themselves.

In an Aboriginal context, discussion of these ideas at the moment revolved around the living standards of the tribal Aborigines, and the prospect of inter-racial marriage, and the character of "half-castes". The concept of assimilation was very much up in the air.

One Last Comment. What did you think, at the time?

OTHER VEXATIOUS MATTERS

There was no shortage of colour issues.

Press report. May 4. The House of Representatives last night voted against extending voting rights to all Aborigines. At the moment, only those Aborigines who were registered to vote in some states, and those employed by the Armed

Services, were entitled to vote. An amendment to the existing Act would have given the vote to all.

The Prime Minister pointed out that he advocated **waiting** until a Select Committee that had been set up to consider voting rights, had made its report. It was clear that he envisaged considerable extensions to those rights, but he wanted to proceed carefully, and do the matter properly in some months.

Comment. The good news was that voting rights had clearly risen to the top of the agenda.

> **Letters, G Hobson.** When I was in Moree Hospital recently for six weeks I noticed that adjoining the main hospital was another large ward for Aborigines with black nurses. What in the world is wrong with this? If any of us were to go to Japan or any other country of a different colour, would we object if there were special hospitals or pubs for such as us? Of course we would not, yet everywhere the authorities are trying to force whites to assimilate blacks. **The birds of different breeds in the bush don't mix, nor do the animals because it is not natural.**

Comment. No comment.

Press report. Darwin. May 16. Judge Joske, of the Northern Territory bench, today held the first session of the newly created Wards Appeal Tribunal. This body was to hear appeals from Aborigines, most of whom **were regarded as wards of the Territory.** The grounds for such an appeal would be that he did not need the special care provided by the Aboriginal Welfare Branch. If an appeal was successful, he would become a full citizen.

The very first appellants for citizenship were Nuggett Dongalgarri, and Jack Mulberry. Nugget told the court that he had been convicted for drinking offences, and had been in trouble for assaulting his wife on occasions. He wanted to be a citizen so that he would not have to live on a reserve. His appeal was rejected.

Mulberry was an upstanding tribesman, and took the oath with great dignity. "I was born **on** Lameroo Beach, just in front of the courthouse, 45 years ago. I went to school for a while, but it was very hard for me to learn. I was too old.

"I sleep in a bed. I have a mattress and sheets and a mosquito net on the bed. I eat at a table. I use a knife, fork and spoon. I have never had a bank account because I did not have enough money. I own nothing except my axe and my clothes."

When asked why he didn't want to be a ward anymore, he replied "I want to be citizen. Being a ward is a very hard thing. I want to live like you people, like the white people".

Judge Joske reserved his decision.

CRACKER NIGHT

Letters, M O'Connor. Last year "cracker night" was the most outrageous and most prolonged for years, which proves that it is growing steadily worse. Air and ferry services had to be suspended and all traffic slowed down, the fog on that night being greatly aggravated by the reckless use of gunpowder. Firemen and policemen, who were called to protect the helpless by putting out fires, were pelted with exploding bungers, eggs and overripe fruit; fireworks were thrown into an elderly woman's home, into shops and buses, and flung about in theatres; one fireman was badly dazed by a blow from hooligans as he was discharging his duty; and fires of old furniture were kindled in the street to the peril of pedestrian and motor traffic.

Surely these senseless outrages have gone on long enough. The old, the sick, the peaceful and good citizens who wish for quiet must be considered, and we ought to protect our protectors – the police and fire brigades. "Cracker night" is a disgrace to Sydney, and that which is abused should be abolished by the enforcement of a law against exploding crackers and making bonfires in public streets, all persons found doing so being liable to arrest.

POMS ON THE LOOSE

Letters, H Jones. It appears to be accepted that in their approach to love and matrimony, the British are more shy and restrained than other peoples.

This view is supported by the fact that there are **thousands of unattached British men and women in our community**. Many of these are lonely but might easily find happiness were it not for our too-formal way of life. Could they not be given some encouragement, say by way of a "Happiness" or "Get Together" week?

KOOKAS ON THE LOOSE

News item. The Royal Society for the Prevention of Cruelty is investigating a complaint that birds are being cruel to a man.

Mr C Sanders, a TPI pensioner of St. Lucia, has complained to the society that his home is being "dive-bombed" by flocks of kookaburras. "They ought to do something about it," Mr Sanders said today. "Laughing jackasses? This is no laughing matter to me. My wife and I are being made nervous wrecks."

He said that at dawn and dusk, 30 kookaburras perch on trees around his home, then dive for a plastic-gauze window near the rear steps. The kookaburras have peppered hundreds of holes in the gauze with their beaks.

"But what gets me is the noise when they strike," Mr Sanders said. "It's like someone hitting a drum.

"If we leave the doors or windows open, the kookaburras get inside the house and start pecking at a big looking-glass in the lounge. They flap around the place breaking ornaments. A lady next door has had glass louvers broken by these bombings."

Prevention of Cruelty Inspectors conferred with Mr and Mrs Sanders at their home yesterday and inspected the damaged gauze window. They offered this possible solution: Leave the doors and windows open, let the kookaburras fly into the house, catch them, and then the Society would take them away.

Mr Sanders does not think much of the plan. "What the heck do they think I am – a trapper?", he said. "Anyway, the birds would wreck the place. I've got a better idea – a .22 rifle. But, of course, these kookaburras are protected by law."

INSANITY AS GROUNDS FOR DIVORCE

Late last year, in my **1960 book**, I showed several Letters from spouses of patients in mental hospitals who **were classified as insane**. Existing divorce laws prohibited them from gaining a divorce on those grounds alone.

A few months ago, uniform divorce laws were brought in across the Commonwealth, and one of the changes was to enable divorce, under certain conditions, on the grounds of insanity.

The conditions imposed by the new Laws were that the respondent must be of **unsound mind,** was unlikely to recover, and had been in a mental hospital for five years. Obviously, there were still some problems that applicants had to face. For example, many psychiatrists were reluctant to say a person would **never** recover. Others would also be reluctant because of the mental stress that could be caused to a patient on being confronted with knowledge of an application.

At the moment, more than 60 patients in NSW were faced with divorce proceedings under the new legislation. Hundreds more applications were expected now that the Court had given a definitive ruling and set guidelines for such proceedings. Many husbands and wives had waited up to 25 years for this situation to be addressed.

A FAST-MOVING WORLD

The outside world was moving at a rapid rate. To show you the never-ending roll-over of overseas events, I have made the list below. It shows some of the bigger international stories covering a period of just five days in late June. I invite you to look at the items, and not worry about what was happening, but rather notice the variety and dispersion of anxiety-points round the world.

REDS TO SEND WARPLANES TO INDONESIA. Russia was always willing to help a friend.

US DILEMMA OVER NEUTRON TESTING. The top warriors were for a **death-ray** bomb.

REBEL FRENCH FARMERS STONE POLICE. Farmers did not want to lose their favoured status.

IRAQ TRIES HER HAND AT IMPERIALISM. Brits leaving after 60 years, Iraq wanting to absorb Kuwait.

KENNEDY WARNS REDS: ALLIES FIRM ON BERLIN. More chest-thumping. '

REDS CALL FOR NAURU SELF RULE. There were 2,546 of them. No prize too small for the Reds.

EICHMANN TELLS OF HITLER'S ORDERS. One of Hitler's favourite Jew-slayers was on trial.

UK ENTRY TO COMMON MARKET. Would we in Australia lose out?

Comment. There was an endless stream of such events from all over. A large number came to nothing.

JUNE: ESMERALDA GOES HOME

News item, June 4. More than 100,000 people yesterday gave the Chilean training ship, Esmeralda, an unforgettable farewell from Sydney. An unprecedented crowd packed every vantage point between Circular Quay and the Heads to watch the four-masted barquentine slowly move out to sea like a great white bird.

There were record traffic jams in harbourside suburbs as cars bound for Watson's Bay and North Head clashed with Saturday shoppers. Hundreds of small craft, the largest armada ever seen on Sydney Harbour, escorted the Esmeralda from her berth in Sydney Cove from 10am. Scores of pretty girls were on the wharf....

LETTERS RE *ESMERALDA*

You might expect that such an earth-shattering event as the departure of a sailing ship would bring forth quite a few Letters. Indeed, you were right. Some of them are below.

Letters, J Watson. Surely the ecstatic, almost hysterical, farewell to the graceful Esmeralda proves that we Sydneysiders are grossly starved of spectacle?

"Rock-and-rollers" may draw the younger, Americanised section of the public, certain sporting fixtures may have a specialised appeal, and the tired banners of the annual Six Hour Day procession may attract a dedicated minority, but it takes almost a Royal visit to stir the great mass of the Sydney public.

Would not both State and Federal Governments, in view of the mounting disrepute and colourlessness of democracy, be well advised to consider the human hunger for a little grandeur in our daily life! We need circuses as well as bread.

Letters, Frank Hurley. J Watson, referring to the "ecstatic, almost hysterical farewell to the graceful Esmeralda," does not in any way prove "that we Sydneysiders are grossly starved of spectacle" or that there is "mounting disrepute" and "colourlessness" in democracy.

What, then, provoked such interest in this ship and her captain and crew? Why do masts and sails make a deeper call than the coming and going of the most modern liner or aircraft-carrier?

At heart we are a nation of sea lovers, and intensely responsive to the spirit of adventure. The sails of the Esmeralda were to most a symbol of 1,000 years of sea lore and of man's eternal challenge of the sea. Men in sailing ships first founded our nation, so is it any wonder that this beautiful **Esmeralda** kindled in all of us that dormant adventurous spirit that ordered life so tends to suppress?

As for "the human hunger for a little grandeur in our daily life," surely our souls are not so dead as not to be thankful for the glorious environments in which we live. **Or are we too satiated by a surfeit of sport?**

For me this visit had special significance. It brought back keenly to mind a day in August, 1916, when a little Chilean trawler, the Yelcho, pushed through icepacks and rescued the marooned men of **the Shackleton expedition** from a rock ledge on Elephant Island. So the wholehearted welcome given to these representatives of the Chilean nation is one in which I enthusiastically joined, for I was one of the rescued!

Letters, J Watson. Frank Hurley's views must always be treated with respect, but I fail to see how he arrives at his conclusion that Australians are a nation of sea-lovers.

If he had watched the departure of the Esmeralda from the same spot as I did last Saturday he would have heard such remarks as "Front end of the boat" yelled above the Americanised music coming from transistor radios in the hands of Australian females whose trousered sterns were far less elegant than the ship's. And the behaviour of the motorized citizenry trying to escape from the North Head peninsula after the spectacle would have shamed a newly liberated Congolese.

I still maintain Sydneysiders are starved of spectacle, and it was this starvation, coupled with the wide Press coverage, which made the visit of the Esmeralda such a success.

Comment. Most of the Letters spoke of the sheer beauty of the ship, and the wonderful pleasure that innumerable families got from the morning. The general opinion was that kill-joys would be better off not commenting.

TEMPERANCE IN ALL THINGS

Temperance Societies in Australia had a long history. They started in Australia in the 1830's with the idea that alcohol should be drunk in moderation, but by the time they reached their hey-day in the 1890's, they stood for complete abstinence. At that time, they were quite a large social force in the nation, and owned and managed several large (non-alcoholic) hotels that became prominent social venues in the cities. They were very conspicuous in Melbourne.

During *WWI*, they had a major success in that they moved the various Governments to prohibit the sale of alcohol after 6pm daily, right across the nation. The idea was to help the war effort because it was argued that later drinking badly affected performance at work the next day. Twenty five years later, in most States, the 6pm curfew was still in place, and the famous six-o'clock swill was very much alive and kicking.

By 1961, the States had modified their drinking laws. NSW is fairly typical. It had held a referendum early in the 1950's to seek a later closing. This was defeated. Later in the decade, closing hours were set at 6.30pm, but the venues re-opened at 7.30pm, and stayed open till 10pm. This was a disaster for everyone concerned, especially hotel owners.

By 1961, most States had 10 o'clock closing. On top of that, the run-down, disgusting conditions in local pubs were being challenged by the new Licensed Club movement.

Rugby Clubs, and Workers, and RSL's, and Bowling and Business-mens' Clubs were starting to be licensed, and drinking conditions were approaching acceptable. In the face of these changes, the number of Temperance Chapters fell off, and so did the number of members.

That did not mean, however, that the zeal of the Temperates had disappeared. Backed up by some Protestant Churches, there was a substantial contingent of rabid believers who were ever ready to spread the message that the consumption of liquor carried many risks. Equally well, there was a host of serious drinkers who saw advantages and pleasures in the moderate consumption of the beverages.

Below are a couple of typical Letters that present some facets of the arguments. Characteristically, the writers are forthright in their statements, and leave you in no doubt about what they think. The third Letter was written by a Peter Kelly, who was at Uni with me. A charming, cultivated man, a true Arts graduate in the old sense, he puts his own peculiar argument in his own peculiar way.

Letters, L Shrubb. I recently discovered that one of the subjects taught at my child's State primary school is "Health and Temperance." The textbook is put out by the Youth Temperance Education Council and Band of Hope Union, NSW. It was last revised in 1957, but not extensively, and appears to have been originally written for the children of industrial England at the turn of the century. Thus, although it names Lorraine Crapp as an abstemious swimmer, its cricket list is something less than contemporary: Dr W G Grace, Victor Trumper, Jack Hobbs, and, finally, Bradman. (Perhaps all other cricketers are fond of a glass.)

The book is full of fascinating information: "Among heavy drinkers 'hob-nailed liver' is a common complaint"; "Members of abstainers" lodges like the Rechabites and Sons of Temperance recover from illness nearly twice as quickly as those belonging to the many non-abstainers' lodges"; "Many evils follow excessive drinking. Carelessness, neglect, waste, poverty, gluttony, riotous behaviour and crime..."; "Wheat will germinate in water but not in alcohol." I wonder would it germinate in, say, tomato sauce, pineapple juice, milk or any one of a hundred other non-alcoholic liquids? And so on.

I do not wish to misrepresent the book: a great deal of it is concerned with things like fresh air, fruit, brushing the teeth, and what to do for fainting and snake-bite. But there is a matter of principle involved – if the Education Department permits school-teachers to spend school hours spreading the word of one (admittedly well-meaning) minority, why does it discriminate against others? Why not a weekly theosophy class? Rosicrucianism? Anti-vivisection? Rationalism? All these groups, and others, have earnest spokesmen. Or is the Temperance Union in a special position because it once commanded a large vote?

It seems to me that matters not in the syllabus should not be foisted upon either children or teachers in time that should be spent on teaching syllabus material. Children who want to learn to play the recorder, or chess, for instance, are dependent on some teacher's goodwill and their own initiative, and must do these outside class times. Surely temperance meetings should be on a similar voluntary basis. As for the health part – the syllabus already provides for this under the resounding title of "Health and Hygiene".

Letters, E Hughes. L Shrubb's main complaint concerning the teaching of health and temperance in State primary schools seems to be, not that the textbook is out of date, but that the subject is taught at all in a State primary school.

He is quite prepared to agree that a knowledge of the benefits of "fresh air, fruit, brushing teeth and what to do for fainting and snakebite" is essential for the children of these times, but that a knowledge of what alcoholic liquor can or cannot do for the health of the children and nation is not essential or beneficial. Is this logical?

He speaks of the principle involved. I wonder has Mr Shrubb considered the principle involved in not letting the children know the true facts concerning alcohol? Should not the children know that, when alcohol is taken with food, the carbohydrates in the food are not used in the normal manner, but are deposited as fat around the heart and abdomen, paving the way for heart and other diseases? Should they not be taught that alcohol retards the nervous system and slows digestion, to name just a few points? Should they not know that they will not become one of Australia's 300,000 alcoholics unless they take the first glass? Prevention is better than cure.

The question of the consumption of alcohol is intimately tied up with the subject of health, and one cannot be taught properly without considering the other. Let us give the facts to the children in the schools, then they can decide for themselves which course to follow.

Letters, Peter Kelly. E Hughes' homily on the evils to health of alcohol demands that he be asked if he has never himself stepped or fallen from the straight and narrow and drunk tea with his meals, eaten toast or crumpets dripping with butter, filled up at a party on pastry or sweets, enjoyed a pipe, a cigarette or a good cigar, risked eye-strain watching a late show on TV, flung carelessly into jeopardy his entire central nervous system, blood pressure and general good health as he listened to an exciting Test in the early morn, or sometime, some place, drunk to the memory of some cobbers who died in a war?

All are dangerous to health; most people indulge such weaknesses, at least in moderation; but if Mr Hughes has never done these heinous things, why bother to stay alive?

BUTTER VERSUS MARGARINE

The butter versus margarine fight was just starting. The whole matter was quite confusing to the end user. On the one hand, you had the butter brigade saying that butter was good for you, and marg was bad. And of course the competitor put out the opposite message.

No one was at all sure what the health situation really was, and perhaps that still remains true in 2020. In NSW and elsewhere, on top of that, butter had a favoured and protected position in the market-place. Basically the Government had said, in its own complicated way, that the sales of marg had to be restricted to the same level as the sales of butter. This was obviously a bias in favour of butter, and it defied any concept of free market competition, and made the distribution of marg chaotic.

Letters, R Jenkins. The Government professes to support the National Heart Campaign – in research at least. On the other hand it denies people the right to eat pure vegetable margarine, which is recommended by doctors for those with a heart condition.

Because this solidified vegetable oil is classified as margarine, the Government rations its production to butter sales. While I agree with the principle, the time has passed for this suppression, particularly since eminent specialists like Dr Paul White advocate non-fat diets.

My heart bleeds for the sufferer who at present has to go from shop to shop to obtain one pound of this precious commodity. I will gladly give 5 Pounds to the Campaign, but how about the Government making it easier for the sufferer to help himself?

Letters, E Pepperdine. I had to make 10 calls on health food stores in three different suburbs to obtain one pound of pure vegetable margarine for my husband, in accordance with doctor's orders.

It is diabolical for a Government to appeal to the "big hearted" public for funds for the Heart

Campaign and at the same time deny heart patients their essential food. It will not make them eat butter at any cost, and such unnecessary dictatorship is a disgrace to Australia.

Letters, W Reid.   R Jenkins' plea for more vegetable margarine is based on a common misapprehension. The reason that vegetable oil is recommended in cardiac conditions is that it is unsaturated fat. However, many people – and, sadly enough, some doctors – are unaware that when vegetable oil is hydrogenated (i.e.solidified by hydrogen gas) it automatically becomes a saturated fat in common with butter, lard and all the fats of animal origin. Thus if butter has any ill effect on the heart – and this has yet to be proved – then vegetable margarine is equally injurious, and many people are pointlessly denying themselves butter which is not only the most delicious but the most digestible of all dietary fats.

Letters, H Smith.   I reject both margarine and butter in my non-fat diet. After all, why worry about scraping something over the two slices of my daily bread? I take valuable vegetable oils by the spoonful, four teaspoonful daily, and now the sparkle is returning to my step, and I am gradually getting back the old feeling that something exciting is going to happen – all of the time.

Letters, E Dark.   Mrs E J Pepperdine needs an answer in the public interest. She, with probably many thousands more, believes that margarine is better than butter for people with disease of the heart and arteries.

Certainly natural vegetable oils are better, but margarine is no longer a natural oil after having gone through the process of being turned into a solid. Mr Reid (above) is right in his arguments against margarine. His statements can be verified in any elementary inorganic chemistry textbook. One of the results of this processing is that margarine, instead of lessening the cholesterol level of the blood, raises it. This consideration doubtless led the "Lancet" to say in a leading article, "The hydrogenation plants of our modern food industry may turn out to have contributed to the causation of a major disease."

MUSIC MAESTRO PLEASE

The Sydney Town Hall, long before the Opera House opened, was a great place for symphony concerts. A big sandstone building, with no end of acoustics and echoes, there was never any problem in hearing the music. But it was a big, friendly, chaotic barn of a place, with entrances to the main hall from the foyers all over the place, and really no pretence of sophistication. I have two striking memories of the place.

The first was when I was a senior Uni student, and had enough money to attend my first symphony. I was with a very cute red-headed girl, and anxious to make a good impression. So, when the first movement of the first piece ended, I wanted to be seen as being in raptures, so I applauded with enthusiasm. It turned out, as you know, that you do not applaud until **the end of the entire piece**, so that meant that myself, and about a dozen other hicks, were the only ones clapping. Of course that meant that the other 990 people there all turned and stared, very smugly, at the small scattering of tyros, and I am sure half of them actually sniffed down their noses at us. It was hard to see the humour of this at the time.

The second was the occasions of the Prom concerts that started in Sydney about 1960. I fancy these wonderful events had their origin in Britain when orchestras played in the London Gardens, and the gentry promenaded up and down. In any case, these were always special nights. All seating was removed from the Town Hall, and everyone brought a cushion, and sat on it wherever they could find room. Dress was much less formal than for normal concerts, and the programme was much lighter. The music was very good, almost toe-tapping stuff. Somehow, everyone was a bit excited, and that got everyone else excited. So a grand night was always had by all. It was much better than being glared at.

There were pitfalls, other than premature acclamation, for the unwary to fall into. One very famous international conductor did his best to get offside with his very own audience.

Letters, H Blum. Last Thursday night, at a concert by the Sydney Symphony Orchestra, the guest conductor, Sir Bernard Heinze, reprimanded the audience after the completion of Walton's 2nd Symphony, and asked it to show appreciation by louder applause.

Together with a number of friends I consider his admonition as being in extremely poor taste, and totally unnecessary. Approval or otherwise of a work given should most definitely be left to the audience, who after all paid to attend the concert and are therefore entitled to voice their own opinion on the work performed by the orchestra.

Letters, (Miss) V Comerford. As one who attended last Thursday's symphony concert at the Town Hall, I am in complete agreement with the opinion expressed by H Blum, that it was somewhat out of place for such a highly renowned musical figure as Sir Bernard Heinze to reprimand the audience in the way he did for its poor applause of Walton's 2nd Symphony.

Never, in all my concert-going experience in England and Europe, have I known a conductor express his annoyance at lack of applause – for noise, late arrival, or inattention, yes, but such is excusable. Walton's ear-splitting and harshly brilliant work is an extraordinary achievement, but would hardly appeal sufficiently to the finer emotions of deeply musical listeners to move them o violent applause. Rather, it has the contrary effect – hence the somewhat shattered silence and feeble applause which did greet both orchestra and conductor at the symphony's finish.

Letters, P Simpson. I was privileged to be in the audience at last Thursday's subscription concert when Sir Bernard Heinze reprimanded the audience for its lack of applause following a fine performance of Walton's Second Symphony.

The behaviour of Sydney concert audiences during recent years has been depressing, and it is to Sir Bernard's credit that he has had the courage to do something about it.

H Blum suggests that because he has paid for his ticket he is not obliged to show appreciation of the performance. If the orchestra members and conductor adopted this mercenary attitude and performed only because they were paid to do so, their performances invariably would be pedestrian, and not worth listening to.

Letter, R Kay. One is entitled to surprise that the conductor of a symphony orchestra should comment at all – and even with indignation – on the absence of that breach of public behaviour – only pardonable when it is uncontrollably spontaneous – which consists in beating the hands together, as do angry baboons.

Surely a musician realises that the full enjoyment of music is in contemplation, and not in exhibitionism.

JULY: STATE FUNDING OF SCHOOLS

At about this time, right across the nation, debate broke out about the extent to which Governments should finance education in non-State schools. A number of suggestions were being brought forward to give money to these schools for books, bursaries and fees, and that would take some of the burden off denominational schools, and share it with the entre community. Since the Catholic Church had an extensive networks of **primary and secondary schools across the nation,** the proposals were seen as being of a great benefit to them, and the losers could have been seen as everyone else.

The main argument advanced by Catholic parents was that public schools did not provide the type of religious education that they claimed for their children. These people wanted education to take place in an atmosphere where prayers were recited a number of times a day, where children went off to church services a few times each week, and where teachers were brothers or monks or sisters from religious orders who were dedicating their lives to providing education with a Christian emphasis.

None of this came with a State school education, and in some cases, teachers in those institutions were decidedly antagonistic to the Christian or Catholic faith. Also highly valued was one period of classroom time each day for teaching the various aspects of Catholicity. So, Catholics often argued that to send children to State schools would be in violation of their faith.

The arguments against this were many and varied. The foremost one was that everyone paid taxes, and a public education system was paid for by these. If Catholics wanted to avail themselves of this system, they were free to do so. But it was wrong to hope that the State would help them to promote a different system that only they could use.

And even if the State did do that, would not the inevitable consequence be that every suburb and town would end up with perhaps four schools, each catering for its own sect? Surely this would be an incredible waste of resources.

Catholics argued back that if the Catholic school network suddenly shut down and all their children went to State schools, the system could not cope, and then the cost of patching up a new system would fall on everyone. And so it should **now** be borne by everyone.

Then, on the other hand, opponents argued that Australia provided for a separation of Church and State, and that would hardly be maintained if the State paid for Catholic schooling.

Arguments in the different States went back and forth, and I could not hope to chronicle them here. What I will do is pull out a few extracts that show the tenor of them, and their intensity, and from them you should be able to gauge just how intractable this question was.

Letters, Robert Innes Kay. Now in a socialist world I am taxed to pay for the schooling – I avoid the word education – of everyone's child, dolt or genius. I put up with this because I am born in a socialist time and place, like it or not.

But even in such a time and place I resent, and hotly, being taxed willy-nilly to pay for two schools in the same suburb; and sometimes in the same street; because the priests of one denomination refuse to accept the offer open to all denominations to give their religious instruction in the Public schools. If there are reasons of faith or doctrine which make this necessary, let there be two schools, or 20 if need, side by side – but not out of my pocket.

Letters, E Gill. We must allow parents to choose the kind of education their children are to receive. Everyone knows that this freedom has been fully preserved in Australia. **We fully approve the right to have church schools.**

The question of State aid is another and more complicated matter. Roman Catholics share in the control of the public system of education, and it is right that all should contribute to it. But to ask for public funds for your own schools and at the same time to have a say in the control of public schools is having one's cake and eating it too.

So we could say they can contract out of taxation for public schools. But where will this stop? If we contract out for Catholic schools, will we be forced to do the same for Communist schools.

Letters, (Rev) W Murray, Director Catholic Information Bureau, Sydney. The principle that parents have a prior right to choose the kind of education their children are to receive is generally recognised. But in exercising this right parents are not free to violate their own conscience before God to Whom they are responsible for the upbringing of the children He has entrusted to them. Children, too have rights, and one of them is the right to a proper upbringing in the faith in which they have been baptised. This upbringing includes their education. So the exercise of parental rights in regard to their children is conditioned by the corresponding rights of their children.

Catholic parents have demanded a Catholic education system for their children in spite of the intolerable financial burden involved, not for the fun of it, but simply because their conscience will not permit them to submit their children to a system of purely secular education.

The Church, entrusted with a divine mission in regard to souls, will always insist that Catholic parents do their duty both in regard to God and in regard to the children He has entrusted to them.

Letters, W McCauley. State education is provided by the people, for the people, in much the same manner as numerous other public services and utilities are provided.

Surely if I as an individual taxpayer should refrain from the use of one or all of these services then that is my own personal choice and my own responsibility. Should I refrain from using public transport would this then entitle me to a tax rebate? Do I get a grant from the Government because I choose to enter a private hospital instead of a public hospital? Should private motorists receive a grant from the Transport Department because they don't use the buses provided?

There is no compulsion on me to have my children educated in a particular type of school, there is only compulsion that I must have my children educated to certain standards and the means to do this is placed at my disposal by the Department of Education. This is very right and proper and I am grateful that my children live in a country where it is so.

Letters, CHILDLESS SPINSTER, Kirribilli. We often read that parents who send their children to private schools are **paying twice for their education**. Well what about the struggling spinster whose tax contributions pay for family allowances, education, and all the other amenities which parents are allowed.

Parents choose to become parents, and they enjoy all the accompanying happiness. They also have children to turn to in later years. Parents should count their blessings, shoulder their responsibilities, and not whinge.

Comment. There was no quick fix available here. The facts of the matter now though are that the pendulum has slowly swung in favour of the "private" schools and that public funds and grants are liberally given to them. This is a battle that still flares up at times, and the same arguments are trotted out. Though to no avail, because no one's attitude is ever changed as a result.

MENZIES ON THE EDGE

Twenty years ago, Bob Menzies **had** been Prime Minister. This was after the start of the European War, and before the start of the Pacific. He only held the position for a few months, and **was then bumped out** when two Independents voted against him on important issues. Needless to say, the memories of being sent back to the Opposition still remained with him, and right now I would expect they were becoming very real in his mind again.

That was because things were slowly shaping up against him. The economy was still drifting badly for him. There were more sackings, and the credit squeeze was biting so hard that he lifted it on June 30. This was one full year earlier than Treasurer Holt had just indicated. Sales of this and that, including wool and steel products, were down. Just generally, the whole economy seemed to be dragging.

On top of that, this Government had been in power for ten years, and had lost the fire in its belly for reform. It was spending its time putting out fires from its earlier initiatives, and not with **new** policy. So the electorate was getting bored and a bit disheartened. And the elections were, at most, five months away. My guess would be that if he does not pull a rabbit out of the hat soon, he will have a miserable Christmas.

THE WOMAN'S PLACE IS IN .... ?

I always argue that the start of modern Womens' Lib was in WWII, when the men went off to war and the women came out and took their jobs. That aside, the 1960's are generally credited in retrospect with having seen many changes in the status of women in the eyes of the community, and in their own eyes. In 1961, there were just a few signs that such a period was in the offing. The Letters below show mainly conservative stances, with just the faint awareness of pastures that might or might not be greener. What do you make of them?

Letters, Judith Davis. I am always distressed to read a letter such as that by Hector McDonald, in which he complains that professionally trained women engaged in home duties are not giving "the community" the benefit of their training.

Ideas are the hard things to come by. And, surely, the woman who has had intensive training in logic, discipline of thought and self-expression is doing a much better service to the community by her creative **training of our future citizens.**

It was once fashionable, in the earlier days of emancipation, for professionally trained women to denigrate home duties, but I think most women nowadays realise that the community is much better served by the education of their children in an intelligent, creative manner than by their transferring land from Bloggs to O'Reilly, or matching up paint samples in a laboratory.

Letters, Marion Hearnshaw. Miss Cleland, who commented in the "Herald" that Australian women were "terribly backward", must number herself among those "backward' women, despite her training and practice as a lawyer, if she considers "child bearing and the role of housewife" inferior to other professions.

Surely the home is the very pinnacle of our social experience and what we need more than anything is a special training and educational motive which will translate the biological experience of motherhood into the highest of all professions.

True, a mother must be free of some of the incessant demands of home management to enter actively into public life, and there is a great need for mothers in public life. But to make this possible for mothers we need a **band of dedicated women as "home associates"** who will be highly trained and qualified in family organisation and home building, with a professional status altogether away from the "situation" attached to the old domestic "servant" which Miss Cleland mentioned.

Letters, Rosemary Howe. The two points of view expressed in your correspondence "Womens' Role in the Community" are too extreme. There are a number of women who are content to stay at home and do not want or need outside interest thrust upon them as a social duty.

Many women resent the present controversy because they use their time constructively and yet are told by the critics, "You are wasting your time at home, you should be employed in the community." There are two real objections to this that no one has bothered to emphasise.

The homemaker genuinely gives her whole capabilities to the welfare of her family and this includes raising funds for her children's schools and other charities which certainly do affect her community life. Who will do this unenviable chore if everyone works? Will her pay cheque go to support charities and not be treated as recompense for personal exertion?

The fact that some women are compelled by necessity or desire to manage a career plus family is established, but let the homemaker busy herself to her own satisfaction without criticism.

Letters, H Maxwell. Your correspondent Rosilyn Baxter, who bemoans her fate as being confined to the mother role, must ask herself the question, "Does she expect the male to be the breadwinner or not?" If she expects the male to be the provider, then she cannot expect a job in preference to the male, and she certainly cannot have it both ways.

It is noticeable also that the female only wants to do the pleasant tasks in life. She has no desire to do her share of the dirty and uncongenial tasks that are the lot of most men, such as emptying the garbage tins. All most women want is to lick off the cream and leave the skim milk to men.

Letters, Homemaker. Rosilyn Baxter asks if "women must boost their ego by emphasising the importance of their peculiarly feminine role," but the fact remains that we are females, and, as such, those who marry and have children must make a home. Surely there can be nothing of more importance to a nation than happy, well-adjusted homes and families, and I will always maintain that in many cases where the mother goes to work the homes are simply boarding-houses.

In the case of a few women who are genuinely interested in public affairs the home life may not satisfy, but the average woman who works does so purely and simply for money, which she spends as fast as she earns. If she stayed at home and use her talents to utilise adequately her husband's wages to the best advantage, the "home" would by much happier, even if the "house" was not quite as well furnished.

I do not "proclaim the sacred role of wife and mother", but the fact remains that, if a woman is a wife and mother, she cannot adequately run a well-adjusted home from an outside job. If she does not stay home and do it properly, she should never have married, a job which requires work if ever one did.

Comment. There was little discussion yet about careers for women, or the rights and wrongs of two-income families or glass ceilings, and so on.

FREE LOVE .... WHACKO

"Here in the Western world, in Great Britain, America, and Australia, even Sydney, we have those who are shamelessly teaching in our universities the same shameless philosophies, that there is no God. Such lecturers are decrying the institution of marriage, urging our students to pre-marital sexual experience, and **advocating free love** and the right of self expression." Thus spake the Primate of Australia, and Anglican Archbishop of Sydney, Dr Gough on July 6th.

He was speaking at the 12th biennial legal convention of the Law Council of Australia, so he could hardly hope to have his comments slip through unnoticed.

Dr V Kinsella, a Macquarie Street specialist, a close colleague of Dr Gough, and the source of Gough's above statement, went on to decry "the menace of the teaching of Sydney Uni's so-called philosophy professors, Anderson and Stout. An entire civilisation can be undermined if men like these are permitted to go unchecked. They are not philosophers. They are sceptics."

One half the population of the nation was appalled. Here we had a learned churchman and a learned medical man talking about advocates of free love teaching immorality at one of the nation's leading tertiary institutions. Shock and horror. What will the world come to? Surely, we'll all be doomed.

What about the other half of the population? Well, they too were appalled. But their shock and horror came from the realisation that half the population took any notice of such claims. What is the world coming to? Surely, if we believe this rubbish, we all deserve to be doomed.

So, a violent controversy started. Professor Stout jumped to his own defence. "I have never, in the whole of the 20 years I have lectured at Sydney Uni, even discussed, let alone advocated, the questions of free-love, extra-marital relations, or trial marriage. I am quite certain that not one of the thousands of students who have attended my lectures would ever say that I had. This applies not only to my formal university lectures but also to my talks to

student bodies and my informal discussions everywhere."
Professor Anderson replied in similar certain terms.

Personal comment. I studied for two years under Anderson
in Philosophy, and under Stout in Moral and Political
Philosophy. I give Stout the credit, if that is what it is, for
having civilised me, and for turning me from a primitive
bumpkin into a thinking and moderate person. But that
aside, in my four-man years of involved studentship under
these Professors, never once was there any discussion at all
of these taboo topics.

Of course, these denials did little to douse the conflagration.
Adding fuel to it was the fact that it centred round
philosophy, which was esoteric, undefined, and arbitrary
(my opinion only). So the matter attracted many Letters
for a few weeks, and much societal comment as well. I
have enclosed below just a few Letters that, for whatever
reason, I thought were interesting.

Letters, (Miss) Kate Moroney. Dr Gough's
admonitions and strictures are a solemn reminder
that part at least of our local Establishment is still
thinking in nineteenth (or even sixteenth) century
terms. The Primate must surely realise that
knowledge, understanding, tolerance, and even
forgiveness of fundamental human behaviour,
have progressed rapidly in the twentieth century
without threat to the fabric of society.

Letters, D Armstrong, University of Melbourne.
We were shocked and amazed to read Archbishop
Gough's statements about Sydney University. It
is our conviction that a university lecturer has the
right to hold and say that there is or that there

is no divine law and that he is entitled to adopt a critical attitude to prevailing sexual mores as well as to defend them. If any attempt were to be made to force him to teach doctrines inconsistent with his beliefs, his right as a university teacher would be grossly violated.

We deplore the Archbishop's attempt to link atheists and libertarians with Communists and Communism. The wowserish tendencies now prevailing in Soviet society have been noticed with great satisfaction by many fellow-travelling clergymen, some of them Anglicans, who have done much more to promote Communism in this country than, say, Professor Anderson, who is largely responsible for the fact that, at Sydney University, Communists have never had any real influence

The attempt to link the names of Professors Anderson, O'Neil and Stout with any kind of impropriety is silly and scandalous and should be met with the strongest possible protest. It is to be hoped that Sydney academics, theists and atheists, libertarians and anti-libertarians, will ignore the archbishop's attempts to interfere with academic freedom and that they will have the integrity to resist any interference with their rights.

Letters, R McDonald, University of New England, Armidale. A well-known phenomenon in the psychology of prejudice is the attributing to a disliked group of any trait that is thought undesirable. A typical example is the attribution of sexual licence to groups such as Negroes, Jews and the like. A textbook example of this is the recent statement by Archbishop Gough, in which, according to the ABC report, he managed to couple "free love" with "Communism". The available evidence suggests in fact that Communists are a good deal more puritanical than we are.

Ideally, university lecturers wish to encourage nothing less innocent than the spirit of free inquiry. From the incident of the Socratic hemlock onwards, just this much has commonly been interpreted as "corrupting the youth." A university which produces a ferment of ideas confers long-term benefits on the society which nourishes it. Those who wish tertiary institutions to produce only well trained but "right thinking" people cannot always recognise this.

Letters, M Mackerras. Dr Gough's opinions, somewhat overstated, show a better understanding of the results of the teachings of the Philosophy Department at the University of Sydney than do the statements of most of his critics.

I accept the assurance of Professor Stout that he has never advocated free love, extra-marital relations or trial marriage. But what the Philosophy Department has done is to question Christian morality at three basic points:

One. Is any morality (other than, perhaps, a pragmatic one) necessary for human society?

Two. Can there be such a thing as absolute right and wrong?

Three. Is morality natural-law-determine and God-revealed or is it man-invented? Most of the Philosophy staff would answer "no" to the first two questions and "man-invented" to the third. By doing so they strike at the fundamentals of Christian morality as Dr Gough can clearly see. They may claim a right to do this but surely they cannot deny that this is what they are doing.

I do not believe that people who reject Christian morals in theory necessarily reject them in practice. Fortunately, a great many such people continue to maintain the Christian practices taught them by their parents. Nevertheless, the denial of the concept of right and wrong must affect the behaviour of some people at least. I submit that Dr Gough has good reason for his general complaint.

Letters, Brian Bailey. Those who have studied in the Departments of Philosophy or Psychology at Sydney University at some time during the past two decades or so know well enough that a few students have taken advantage of the free-expression attitude encouraged in these departments.

It was a university joke in my undergraduate days that weekend conferences with high-sounding study titles were used by some as a "blind" for the sort of activity the Primate has in mind.

On the other hand, it is as unfair of the Primate to use a public occasion to condemn this tiny minority as it would be for a professor to condemn in a public lecture those of the Archbishop's priests who teach their people doctrines contrary to the formularies of the English Church.

Letters, A Stout, Professor of Philosophy, Sydney University. Let me say that the courses in philosophy and the textbooks and recommended reading do not differ in any notable respect from those of the other Australian universities or from those of most British universities. A comparison of the handbooks of the various universities would show this.

As for our staff, we have on it graduates of many different universities, including Oxford, London, Louvain, Adelaide, Melbourne, Otago, Wellington and Princeton, as well as Sydney. Two of them, incidentally, are Roman Catholics. The staff members of all university departments are competitively selected for appointment only after wide advertisement in Australia and overseas.

If the entire Sydney philosophy staff were to be dismissed tomorrow and replaced by a new one, the general position would be exactly the same as it is now. The new members might be more able or less able philosophers, but they would be teaching much the same sort of courses and using much the same textbooks.

Once this fact is recognised, I suspect that the attack will turn on the existence of university departments of philosophy at all, and thus ultimately on academic freedom itself. When it does, I shall be happy to reply to it.

AUGUST: COMMON MARKET FOR OZ?

August was always Budget month. And so it was this year. Harold Holt, the Treasurer, brought down multiple sets of numbers, and talked a lot about them, but the net result was very little change. There were a few minor taxes cut, and pensions were increased just a little. But the various pensions and unemployment benefits were still well short of the Basic Wage, and it remained a mystery how people were supposed to survive on them.

August this year was also a big month for policy concerns at all three levels of Government.

THE COMMON MARKET

There was one major problem looming for the Feds. The Brits were getting keener and keener on joining the Common Market. That meant they would enter into all sorts of agreements, with countries of Europe, about the goods they would produce and market, and what they would import, and the tariffs involved. It also meant that they would probably allow freer entry to and from Britain for continental European people who wanted to migrate to Britain. Australia already had preferential treatment from Britain in these matters, but it was quickly becoming clear that Oz would not be a participant in the new arrangements.

So, the question, that was just being formulated, was what would happen to our trade and relationships with Britain. This was a huge question for this nation, because so much of our trade, and so much of our migration, depended on mutually preferential arrangements with the Old Country.

So Menzies and Holt, and McEwen the Trade Minister, were talking a lot about the matter, but little by little the picture seemed to be getting grimmer for this nation. Mc Ewen was of the opinion that Britain's entry without adequate safeguards for us would mean **nothing but havoc**. He warned that there were "able and sophisticated propagandists who are spreading the idea that a prosperous European bloc will somehow mean greater wealth for everyone, including the Commonwealth. **This idea can be exploded in a sentence**." He warned that at the moment, the Common Market Treaty proposed would keep most of Australia's products out of Europe and Britain.

One gentleman below saw things differently.

> **Letters, Theo H Thorne.** I was amazed to read in your issue of August 22nd that a supposedly responsible Minister of the Government like John McEwen, Minister for Trade, should state that Britain's entry into the Common Market would mean "nothing but havoc" for many of Australia's primary industries.
>
> There is no evidence whatever to warrant such a statement, which is born of a negative attitude of mind and a failure to appreciate the **tremendous vista of future world harmony** for which the Common Market is the prelude.
>
> Australia's position was put in a statesmanlike way by W C Wentworth, who said that the change would mean "a painful deployment" of Australia's primary industries, a deployment which will strengthen our national economy by spreading it over vaster areas and in new regions which we

never worried about before because of an easy business with the homeland.

Comment. I think Mr Thorne was being a bit hopeful. He was arguing that as a nation we would benefit by being **forced** to find new markets. This may or may not be true in the long run, but it was not a good prospect for producers who already had old markets. For example, our butter exporters might end up with markets in Africa, say, in five years' time. But that did not seem like a good swap for their existing markets.

This was developing into a huge issue for Australia, and for every nation in Western Europe. In each of these, hundreds of pressure groups were starting to use whatever influence they had to mould developments in the way that would benefit themselves. Take the farmers in France. They had no wish at all to see Australian butter and beef flooding into Europe and Britain. So you could bet that they were covertly or overtly jockeying to keep these products out. On the other hand, they would be happy to see Australia buy more French wine.

At the moment, negotiations were under way. That meant that all the issues were **just starting** to be raised by the various players, so that in fact any concrete moves were a few years away. Right now, however, people here in Oz were getting anxious, and so too was the Government. This issue will come more and more to the forefront over the coming months.

THE STATES TOO WERE TROUBLED.

Each of them was somewhere in the process of deciding what changes it wanted to make to its High School system. In NSW, the Wyndham report had recommended, five years ago, that secondary students in future attend school for six years rather than the current five. There were several good reasons for this. For example, it was often felt that youngsters were getting to university at too young an age. It was also thought by many that current High School courses were too much dictated by passing exams, and not so much by giving a rounded education.

On the other hand, again **as examples**, it was feared that the extra sixth year would not provide a higher standard, and that it would only spread five years of education over six years. Another worry, for a few, was that there would be an increased number of girls who would get pregnant in the final year, and then miss out on the Leaving Certificate as a result.

In NSW, and elsewhere, such changes were a hot issue. Many different schemes were being proposed with their own supporters. Lots of syllabi were on the drawing board, universities were wondering about the hiatus-year that would come with their implementation. About a month ago, the NSW government said that it definitely would introduce the scheme, probably next year. Then in early August, it announced that it had changed its mind, and the start date might be later. So, it all went back up in the air.

Nevertheless the changes, whatever they would end up being, were generally popular with the voters, and they looked certain to come sooner or later.

WYNDHAM ISSUES

Proposals that tried to amend the existing High School system of education had ramifications right through every aspect of society. I cannot hope to cover the many facets and twists and turns of the various moves by the hundreds of pressure groups and individuals. All I can do is give you a tiny selection showing what a couple of people wanted to say, and hope you get an idea of the diversity and enormity of the rethinking that the suggested changes required.

Letters, D Mellor. Critics of the Wyndham Report who advocate an external Intermediate examination be conducted in much the same way as the present Leaving Certificate probably do so on the basis of two assumptions: first, that in a public examination of this kind, candidates are measured with **a uniform measuring-stick**; second, that since the identity of a candidate is unknown to the examiner, there is **no question of bias** in marking the papers.

Few will question the correctness of the second assumption but the same cannot be said about the first. The number of candidates for an external Intermediate Certificate would now be so large and the time available for marking examination papers so short that it would be extremely difficult, if not impossible, to maintain a uniform standard of marking. On balance, it is doubtful whether, in these circumstances, much is gained by an external examination.

If, however, there must be an external examination, one compromise worth examining is that the Board of Secondary School Studies should conduct an Intermediate Certificate examination as it does the Leaving Certificate, except that the marking of the papers would be done by the schools themselves. This would ensure uniformity to the extent that all candidates would be tested with the same examination paper.

Letters, H Gibbs.   The Wyndham Report recognized the futility of the Intermediate Certificate and eliminated it, but the government has succumbed to pressure and has retained it.   The reason given for the retention is that there will be many children forced by economic hardship to leave school at 15 years of age and these children will need a certificate to prove scholastic attainment.

The further proposal that an external examination should be set is under consideration; the argument in support of this being that an external examination would give the certificate some standing and "help children to enter apprenticeships and other specialized employments."

That any child should be denied one more year in school is tragic, and the child who will suffer most is the less bright child who, as Dr Darling says, needs more teaching, not less, to fit him to compete with his fellows. To be provided with the alternative inferior certificate will not help him at all.   He will find that it is a useless document because he will be competing with increasing numbers completing the fourth year Leaving Certificate.

State assistance in cases of real hardship is such an obvious answer that one wonders why it was not proposed. One suspects that the real reason for the retention of the Intermediate Certificate is the inflexible attitude of some people concerned with **the apprenticeship system**, which demands that a child shall leave school at 15 or 16 or miss out. If this is the case, the apprenticeship system should be reviewed and overhauled at once. It is archaic and should have gone out with the "drummer boy."

The age limits have not changed for more than 50 years and bear no relation to modern needs. The courses are the longest in the world and could be cut, in many cases by at least half, if properly streamlined.

LOCAL PROBLEMS.

Local Councils and water-supply authorities were also pondering whether to fluoridate water supplies for domestic use. The NSW Director of State Health Services said on August 8th that he expected fluoride to be introduced in most areas of the State "in a short while." He went on to say that experience overseas indicated a 60 per cent drop in tooth cavities could be expected as a result.

The Opposition spokesman for Health said that, while he did not oppose the chemical being added, it was true that the decision to fluoridate was a local matter and various local authorities had to approve the plan. It was obvious that quite a few local authorities were not yet convinced of the need for such a move, and that it might take a few years before it was universally accepted.

Letters, V Kelly. The easy assurance by the Director of State Health Services, Dr E S Meyers, that water fluoridation "can do no harm" is not shared by some eminent members of his profession. Professor Sir Stanton Hicks has warned that sodium fluoride interferes with the normal functioning of the thyroid gland. Dr W H Hill, Medical Officer for Health, Calgary, Alberta, Canada, has pointed out the strong affinity of sodium fluoride for calcium and the power of the former to make bones brittle.

The Canadian Minister for Health (Dr McKinnon Phillips) has warned that fluoride hardens both arteries and bones, making the latter brittle and likely to fracture readily. Water fluoridation has been condemned by Dr Hugh Sinclair, Director of Human Nutrition, Oxford University, Dr Royal Lee, of the Lee Foundation for Nutritional Research, Milwaukee, and may other responsible medical men.

The medical profession frequently warns the public not to take medicine indiscriminately or to prescribe for their own ailments, yet Dr Meyers is now advising the entire population to be prepared to drink fluoridated water, the physiological action of which at different ages and in differing states of health and the capacities for absorption and elimination are still a mystery.

Water fluoridation is a form of compulsory mass medication and a violation of every person's basic personal freedom to obtain pure drinking water and not medicine when they turn on the tap.

Letters, W Sheahan, Minister for Health, Sydney. I would like to assure Mr V H Kelly and all members of the community that the recent statement by Dr E S Meyers, Director of State Health Services, has the full approval of my Department and the Government, which in 1957 passed the Fluoridation of Public Water Supplies Act.

Fluoridation of water is accepted as an effective, safe and practical public health measure to aid in the control of dental caries, by very many **national health authorities** of the United States of America, the United Kingdom, Canada, Australia and other countries, and also by the World Health Organisation. It was accepted by the Government of this State only after very careful and full consideration of all the factors involved.

I would suggest to the community that they should heed the opinions of persons competent in the field of public health, rather than those of a small minority of persons who are unable to assess objectively these matters which are so important to our common interest.

Letters, J C Walsh, B Sc (Med.). We are indeed fortunate to have such gentlemen as V H Kelly to warn us of the follies of scientific research, but I cannot fully agree with some of the points in his letter.

The concept of water fluoridation stems from observations in the United States that the teeth of children in localities where drinking water contained unusually high concentrations of fluoride (e.g. five parts per million) were particularly resistant to dental decay.   Numerous water supplies in the United States and Great Britain now include sodium fluoride at a concentration considerably lower than many natural water supplies, namely, one part per million.   This procedure has produced a statistically significant reduction in dental decay.

I would point out that the daily intake of fluoride necessary to influence normal bone structure or the metabolism of the thyroid gland is grossly beyond this therapeutic level. It is quite untrue that at these levels, "the physiological action.... and capacities for absorption and elimination are still a mystery."

Comment. As we look back from 2020, fluoridation has been so widely accepted that we almost forget there was resistance to it. But there was considerable doubts about its safety, and its effects, in some regions, and the arguments back and forth raged for another ten years.

IT'S A ZOO OUT THERE

It seemed that animals were in the news this month. Every day the papers carried some wild or silly or worrying article or Letter. In general, these excerpts suggest that animals were a bunch of losers.

News Item. Crocodile shooting is booming in the Northern Territory since the price for skins rose to a record level because of the growing demand for the hide for shoes and handbags.

Two Darwin shooters have just delivered skins worth 2,500 Pounds which they collected in six weeks. Another man shot 400 Pounds worth in four nights after spending 35 Pounds to charter an aeroplane to survey billabongs.

A skin buyer, Mr N J Haritos, said today this season was expected to the best for many years. At least 60 shooting parties are operating in the rivers and creeks between the western border of Arnhem Land and the West Australian border. They are expected to bring in a record **30,000 skins** worth 250,000 Pounds.

Southern buyers are also offering 5/- an inch for freshwater crocodile skins which previously were unsalable. Most skins are exported to France and the Far East for the fashion trade.

Letters, Helena Winter. Killing of **cats** by the RSPCA has not solved the problem of what to do about the unwanted and sometimes difficult-to-catch stray cats in Sydney. Money spent in the collecting and killing of these animals could be more honestly spent in **preventing cruelty,** which is the society's avowed function and which is there for everyone to see in the circus, zoos, stock trains, abattoirs, poultry farms, markets and bird shops – in fact, wherever animals and birds are exhibited or sold for monetary gain.

The law states animals kept in captivity shall have enough room for exercise. Everywhere you see

birds standing about in small cages. Birds were meant to use their wings for exercise. You can see fish in glass jars no larger than a tumbler. Many zoo animals stand about miserably in cages until they die. The exercise the circus animal gets is to perform unnatural tricks under fear of the lash.

How about leaving the collecting and killing of stray **dogs** and cats to the various Councils? How about making it compulsory to register cats as well as dogs and pay one Pound a year registration fee and five Pounds a year for a breeding animal? This money could be set aside for a free animal hospital where people could get their pets desexed free of charge and where a ward could be used for animals with infectious diseases such as mange and distemper.

Letters, E MacLaurin. I am writing to warn all who own dogs that they should keep them chained during such times as they are not being supervised. I had a sheep-dog, with a beautiful coat, on my farm at South Creek; I found his body on Monday in one of the paddocks, with the skin neatly removed. There should be very stringent restrictions on the sale and use of firearms and ammunition if our native creatures and pets are to be saved from destruction by vandals.

Letters, Alma Kingsmill. It is high time the thinking public rose up against the senseless, evil practice of importing animals for the circus.

It is sickening to think of baby elephants being dragged from a warm jungle and collapsing from fright and dying from the effects of a change of temperature; of magnificent lions and tigers crouching in small cages, bears dancing ridiculously at the end of a chain, etc., and all for the entertainment of a nut-crunching, gum-chewing audience.

Letters, Bogue Atkinson, Sydney. From what I know of the RSPCA, I feel that the actual destroying of cats and dogs is carried out in a humane manner. This might not be the case if every Council made its own arrangements.

However, there can be little question that the main function of our animal protection societies is to collect and destroy, as distinct from endeavouring to educate the community to care for, and make secure, the animal's existence.

I suggest that we need some community movement by the people who matter most to us – the social leaders, the "names", and of course by the Churches and its leaders – to teach that the care of animals is a social obligation, and should not just be left to the kinder hearts: to make people feel that the sight of lost, hungry, or sick dogs on our streets, or of mangled sheep in a stock train, is more than just part of our everyday lives, but is concerned with the health of the soul of the community.

Letters, L Corbet, Alice Springs. I do hope that the bird lovers of the Commonwealth will protest strongly against the suggestion that the wild geese on the South Alligator River be thrown to the mercy of a few trigger-happy tourists, anxious to shoot their way round Australia. Let us develop our tourist potential on a higher plane.

Letters, S Robinson. Anyone who has had anything to do with animals at all knows that the only method of training them is first of all by understanding them, and then by infinite patience in showing them what is to be done and by rewarding them for doing it correctly.

Ask an instructor of police-dogs, or a stableman, or a shepherd – they will all reply that not only do they not use cruelty in training, but that cruelty does not pay. They will also say that **a trained animal is a much happier one** than an animal left to its own devices.

Is it not at least possible that most circus animals are happier – they are certainly better fed and cared for – than in the wilds where nature is red in tooth and claw?

BATTLE OF THE SEXES

Letters, J Ankers. When I was younger, a pregnant woman, on realizing that she was in an "interesting condition," would discreetly retire from public view instead of brazenly flaunting her condition as a means of gaining preference.

As for old age not being venerated, on passing the fortieth milestone, we **were** all prepared to grow old gracefully. Nostalgic are the memories of placid white-haired grandmothers, of their black silken dress, jet beads, cameo brooch, velvet neckband. Vestiges of noble womanhood – ludicrous, paint-raddled creatures who, in their matador pants, try to emulate their moronic or delinquent rock-an-roll- granddaughters.

Women who complain about the lack of respect paid to them have only themselves to blame. In copying the men, and following masculine pursuits, they can expect no privileges whatsoever.

Letters, Margaret Harries. I cannot sit back and allow Richard Ankers' letter to rouse me to the fury it does without making a protest.

Mr Ankers must have been leading an incredibly sheltered life since, say, the early 1900s. In those days, the grandmothers of his acquaintance, and mine, sat in their black silks and velvets, enabled so to do because they employed several servants (for a fraction of a living wage) to wait on them and minister to their every need.

There are few of us now who can afford to pay for what is euphemistically called "help" in our homes. And if we do employ people to run our house who do it efficiently, with pride in their work, the wage they receive, and earn, is astronomical.

So how can a pregnant young woman avoid fighting her way in public transport to buy the food which she will carry home, prepare and cook for her husband and, probably, children?

Mr Ankers is in the wrong decade, if not the wrong century! And as well he is without the bowels of human kindness. And from kindness, all good manners spring.

Letters, (Mrs) V E Hanies. The pregnant woman of two generations ago had numerous maiden aunts and sisters to help with chores and shopping. Today, despite the increasing number of large stores in the suburbs, every mother knows that to purchase the correct size shirt, blouse, trousers, shoes, etc., for Tom, Dick, Mary or Jane she has to make a tiring, strap-hanging trip to town as the local stores do not carry a large range of sizes. Also the end-of-season sales in town afford an excellent opportunity to save several pounds, which will help pay off the house a little sooner.

Letters, Dorothy Seldon. To grow old gracefully we need tolerance – a tolerance of a changing world, fashioned by your correspondent's generation – a tolerance in which he is sadly lacking; for to label all today's youth as "moronic and delinquent" and all today's grandmothers as "painted and raddled" is not only intolerant but downright wicked.

I was raised in an era when it was the accepted thing to stand for anyone older or less able than you – and although I have passed the milestone mentioned, I shall continue to do so, without weighing pros and cons, while Richard Ankers and those like him cling grimly to blurred images of the past – and the seats they have grabbed and intend to retain at all costs.

SEPTEMBER: NUCLEAR BOMB SCARES

The Americans and Russians had for the last two years agreed that they should reduce their expenditure on arms manufacture and should also reduce their stockpiles of atomic bombs. Of course, neither of them did this, but each put up a facade of doing so, and reassured the world that they were all for disarmament. So every now and then the leaders would talk about getting together to earnestly discuss their noble aims, while at the same time going crazy on research on neutron bombs and developing vast underground nuclear testing facilities.

On September 1ˢᵗ, the Russians announced that they would resume nuclear testing. They did so with a half dozen explosions over ten days, and then stopped for a while. This threw the Western World into frantic political and diplomatic activity, and for a few weeks the news overseas was obsessed with things atomic.

For example, in America a great rush developed to buy A-bomb shelters. It was reported that the first spate of buyers had bought out stocks in all States, and that the wait-time for new stocks of the more expensive types would be about three months. In the meantime, the cheaper ones would be available in one month, and after that the pricey ones would be ready so that the switch to more expensive ones would be trouble-free.

Various Government Departments argued about a bomb attack from Russia. Would it cause 50 million deaths or would it be 70 million deaths? President Kennedy added to the joy and announced that the fate of mankind would be settled in the next ten months, and that the repercussions of this period would be felt for the next 10,000 years. The Canadian Prime Minister Diefenbaker solemnly said that this was the worst crisis the world had faced since the Second World War.

In Britain 1,966 marchers, who were appealing to world leaders to BAN THE BOMB, were arrested and charged for **disturbing the peace!** In Australia, the reactions were more muted, but even here we had newspapers earnestly printing blueprints for the home-manufacture of fall-out shelters. These came with words of wisdom that advised readers that the worst devastation occurred within twelve feet of the point of impact of the bomb.

Generally, though, the response in Oz was quite lethargic. Some small percentage of the population thought that the danger of war was very real and very frightening, and I expect that even today they think that was so. But most days, the peace-threatening news was on **page three** of the daily newspapers, and most people slept well.

The two Letters below give an indication of the Oz level of concern.

Letters, J Feltwell. With the news that the Soviet Union is resuming the testing of nuclear weapons, it would not be amiss to become parochial and consider this State and its attitude, both as regards words and deeds, and its ability to survive in the event of a nuclear war.

All political parties pay lip service to the policy of decentralization, but if the State Government was working for a future enemy, nothing it could do could be more beautifully performed than the presentation of a concentrated target such as Sydney. We are told that a submarine could surface off Sydney, lob a couple of bombs on the city, and the place could be written off. Any plans to evacuate the population must be chaotic, so lopsided is our distribution of population.

Doing nothing to relieve the situation, the State blames the Federal Government for supplying insufficient money to organize civil defence and states that the public is apathetic towards the matter.

I ask whether the public can be expected to be serious on the subject of civil defence, or show any interest, with the above example before them. Surely the whole key to civil defence is to disperse the target, in other words, decentralization. Instead, it becomes almost a crime to live outside Sydney. The people in the country are slugged to make Sydney a bigger and better target.

Letters, Roy Smith. I must comment on the article "Civil Disobedience, A Problem In UK", and to put one or two things rather differently, perhaps more accurately.

A very large section of the British people **are** actively concerned at the nuclear "policy" pursued by their Government. Rightly so, their campaign receives publicity in accord with its size and influence, and this continues to grow.

Desperate times sometimes call for, and justify, desperate measures. In the struggle to focus attention on the bankruptcy of the "H" bomb policy, the "Committee of 100" is rendering mankind a service. It is always easier to confirm, to agree, to remain silent and do nothing. To speak out often demands the greatest courage, even in today's democracies.

Young people are caught up in such a movement because it has appealed to the young more than any other issue has in postwar Britain. The suggestion by your staff correspondent that snobbish associations with the famous are responsible fall far short of the mark. These people are self-sacrificing of time and energy, and with the "not so young" are trying to bring mankind in their part of the world to an awareness of the horrors of an atomic age.

Would that such a movement be formed in Australia and in every country in the world. Perhaps then we could instil some degree of sanity into our politicians.

WOMEN IN POLITICS

NSW State elections were due in early 1962, and a Federal election had been called for December 9th. Prior to now, only the occasional woman had made it into parliamentary politics, and very few had tried. This time round, in keeping with the accelerating desire for equality and independence, a few more women were talking about throwing their bonnets into the ring.

Letters, F Simon, J Ward. We have read with great pleasure in recent weeks that a number of women are candidates for preselection for the 1962 State elections.

We know that many women are increasingly resentful of working in the auxiliary, money-raisin role in political parties and voluntary organizations where they are denied a voice in policy matters.

Consequently, we hope that the political parties will give due consideration to these women's claims to preselection and not dismiss them because they feel that a woman is a risky candidate.

Letters, Nancy Bird Walton. What nonsense it is to suggest that the two capable women who are offering themselves for the State elections should be excluded because their husbands are already in Parliament! What better training could they have had for the job? I know many politicians' wives who have contributed greatly to the success and work of their husbands.

We do not object to husband-and-wife teams in the other professions. There are doctors, lawyers, teachers and business partnerships, so why not parliamentarians?

Letters, Dorthy Darnell. As an English newcomer I have always been reluctant to voice comments on the local scene which might sound like criticism.

However, the letter on women in Parliament stated more or less what I have been thinking ever since I came to Australia. Compared with England, where women take a considerable part in public life, this country seems very conservative. Considering how early and easily women here got the vote, it is amazing that, politically speaking, they have so little to say.

I therefore sincerely hope that this situation will improve in the near future.

Letters, S. Cross. As a man I applaud the various women who are willing to stand for election to Federal Parliament. I have no doubt that they will get many votes from women just for being a woman. Good luck to them.

I hope though that they campaign on matters that are important to the nation, and do not revert to earlier days and do silly things like chaining themselves to lamp-posts. That will alienate all men and most women. If they are thoughtful and sensible, and are prepared to accept responsibility, they will beat half the men in Parliament now, and bring fresh thinking to the position.

Comment. Many similar Letters over the months welcomed women. Half of them were from men, who were generally of the opinion that the men in Parliament were not doing a good job, and that it was high time for women to be represented as a body. A noticeable number of men said it was **the duty** of women to stand, and they should no longer shirk that responsibility. It will be interesting to see in December just how many women get through **the pre-selection ballots** in the vicious politics of our two-party system.

TRIVIA

In writing this series of books, every now and then a Letter comes through about something completely irrelevant. It's a wonder it gets published at all. Then, for some reason, responses start to flood in. These too are pure nonsense and if they were never written, no one would know or care or be any the wiser or dumber. This month one such initial Letter made it past the Editor, and the thoroughly unenlightening responses were thoroughly entertaining.

Letters, C Lange. Could some of your readers give me a cure for getting rid of the small lizards about three or four inches long which roam around brick walls? They wriggle all mortar out with their tails. I patch it up and they then start somewhere else, where the mortar is soft. They are beginning to get very troublesome.

Letters, S G Redman, Richmond. C Lange asks for a cure to get rid of the lizards that are destroying his brick walls. He should treat the walls with a mixture of mortar and broken-up light globes. When the lizards next attempt their demolition work they'll soon see the light and – well, that's the end of the tail.

Letters, J Riley I suggest that C Lange install a cat – six months old and fun-loving – in his home. Show the cat the little lizards and they will gradually disappear; though the house and grounds will be strewn with lizardless tails and tail-less corpses for some time to come. I write from my own sad experience as I am fond of lizards.

Letters, Ella McFadyen. As one who has observed, and even domesticated, lizards for years, I can assure C Lange that those little garden skinks are protecting his wall, not harming it. It is the small black ants that pick out the mortar from between the bricks. They are the chief food of small lizards, and the skinks are on the wall to feed on them.

The same lizards have often cleaned up an invasion of ants seeking the kitchen, for it is better to employ nature's controls than to fly to poisons, with their harmful chain of later reactions. A little bushy cover below the affected wall, and a sunken drinking vessel, very shallow, will encourage the lizards to render their help.

Letters, H Wolfenden. I have read with interest recent correspondence in your columns concerning lizards.

It is perhaps not generally known that in the remoter parts of the Yorkshire dales, specially constructed "lizard walls" are maintained in connection with a thriving cottage industry.

Long ago, Dalesmen discovered that the minute contractions of a lizards' skin, as it moves about in masonry joints, reduce the mortar to a fine granular substance with flow characteristics far superior to those of sand – in fact, an ideal material for use in eggtimers. Surely there is scope for aldermanic overseas research here in order that a similar cottage craft might be established in Sydney?

Letters, Zoologist. C Lange's lizards which "wriggle all mortar out with their tails" apparently belong to the rare species of rasp lizards (Lacerta raspatoria Youkamel). He would be well advised to contact the Australian Museum, College Street, Sydney.

Letters, Alma Kingsmill. Most of the damage to mortar between bricks is caused by slaters, which work at night: Lizards merely take up residence in the holes made by the slaters.

We have hundreds of lizards in our garden – all harmless. Two of them, "Bill" and "Liz", live in a "split-level" dwelling under the paving and to protect them from our cat we have placed a metal grille over the entrance.

Letters, K Brownscombe. Why blame lizards, slaters or ants for damage to lime-mortar joints in brickwork when it is really due to our salt-laden nor'-easter and southerly winds?   These creatures choose to live there only because it is comfortable.

The erosion usually occurs on windswept walls, especially where sheltered from rain, such as under eaves, where the salt deposited by these winds accumulates and is not washed away by rain.

Possibly the best way to arrest the trouble would be to apply one of the many clear repellants made for water-proofing brickwork.

Letters, (Mrs) E Parmentier.   Mr C Lange is really worried about these lizards in his wall, why doesn't he ask the CSIRO for help? He should send a lizard and a portion of the wall, of course.

Letters, C Lange. (Mr Lange wrote the first lizard Letter.) I will only be too happy to show any person interested about 50 Pounds damage done to my cottage by lizards wriggling out the mortar between bricks with their tails.

Comment. Don't say I didn't warn you.

PUBLIC LAVATORIES

At the end of September the *SMH* quizzed ten American couples, who were each spending about a month visiting many venues right around Australia, what they thought of Australia. The results showed many complaints about our rail travel, and about the lack of fresh food on the breakfast menus of hotels. Room service was poor, and everything about our country hotels was terrible. In particular, the lavatories in the pubs and elsewhere were at the top of the list for criticisms.

When the article was published, several writers added their own views.

Letters, G Macpherson, Nottingham, England. Admittedly in England it may cost a penny, but public lavatories and washroom facilities are available (by law) in cafes, restaurants and all public places. In Sydney, after the stores were closed, in a good-class (they would claim first-class) catering establishment with six waitresses and seating 100 people, we were recommended a theatre some 200 yards away! Does the city

Council of Sydney have no concern for public hygiene?

We are tourists on a round-the-world-trip, and we will rank Sydney in its public services comparable with any backward, underdeveloped and non-tourist-conscious nation.

Letters, Fed-Up. On Tuesday I visited Wynyard's "ladies' room" to see whether it had been improved after all the renovations there. I found the wash-room facilities a disgrace – black, stained and worn-out basins and leaking old taps such as have existed there for years.

What must overseas tourists think of our filthy set-up and entire lack of hygiene?

Letters, Citizen. As a layman, I have long felt that public lavatories generally in this country are unpleasant, badly kept and offensive to the senses; as a doctor, I am convinced of their menace to public health.

I should like to cite two outstanding examples: One male lavatory at Sydney Showground which I visited last week was dirty, odorous and obviously unattended.

Newspaper was lying around in profusion in the cubicles, and the experience upon entering the place was as revolting to anyone's decency as it was dangerous to one's health.

A year ago I took an overseas visitor to see Echo Point, Katoomba. I was appalled and ashamed of a country which tolerated the dungeon-like, foetid atmosphere and totally inadequate facilities. To reach them, one had to descend a dark, dismal stairway and to a dank, nauseous cellar with flies multiplying in glorious abandon. Washing facilities in the male lavatories were totally absent. I understand that the female lavatories were equally repelling.

Why is it that the bodies which control these areas are not more conscious of their responsibilities in the direction of public health? Does Katoomba not have a health inspector?

HUMPTY DOO RICE

Letters, G Bailey. Many warnings from political and business leaders, including prominent overseas visitors, have emphasized the urgent need of diversifying our production for export and exploring new markets, especially in Asia, to offset the falling European market.

In view of this, the collapse of the Humpty Doo rice-growing project is all the more disastrous, especially as the type of rice grown there is the type most sought for in places like Hong Kong.

A few men have remained at Humpty Doo in the rather forlorn hope of retrieving something from the wreck. These men are not optimistic about the prospect of coping with the main cause of the failure – the wild geese. These birds come, not merely in flocks, but in clouds.

Other difficulties are not insurmountable. The rice grew splendidly and prospects for an expanding industry were good, apart from the geese. Every conceivable device has been tried to protect the crop, but to no avail. Nothing but a national approach has any hope of success.

Endeavours to scare the birds off or even to shoot them are naturally futile. But surely it is an incredible situation for a country desperately looking for new export production to allow a most promising industry to collapse for want of a determined national effort to protect it.

The thought does suggest itself that the birds themselves – canned or frozen – might become a profitable export.

Comment. Humpty Doo initially caught Oz imagination. Ever since **WWII**, after the Japanese threat of occupation of our North, there had been calls for us to populate our vast areas of north Western Australia and the Northern Territory. There were hundreds of really silly ideas floated over the years, but ten years ago the idea of irrigating land from rivers, like the Ord and Victoria, took hold, with the aim of building big agricultural enterprises in the region. Eventually, a rice growing project was started at Humpty Doo in 1954. This was scarcely the idyllic picture of man conquering the wild north, because it was only 40 miles out of Darwin. Still, it captured the nation's imagination, and got a lot of government support.

Sadly, by 1962, it had officially failed, because mainly of Frankie Lane's wild geese. It is now growing mangoes very well.

MRS AENEAS GUNN

Mrs Gunn died recently. She was famous in Australia for two books, *We of the Never Never*, and *The Little Black*

Princess. They tell of childhood in the Northern Territory about the turn of the Twentieth Century.

Her first name was Jeannie, but she married a gentleman called Aeneas Gunn, and took his full name when she was publishing. Born in 1870, she was a small woman, only five feet tall. She married Aeneas in 1901, and they sailed to Darwin. Sadly, he died of malarial dysentery just over a year later, and she returned to Melbourne. *The Never Never* had sold over one million copies by the year 1990. It was made into a movie in 1982.

Comment. Speaking as a lad who read these books in primary school, they were wonderful books. They were, incidentally, the only two books in our impecunious small coal-mining school's library.

OCTOBER: MENTAL HEALTH

In 1955, the Federal Government had given substantial grants to Victoria and NSW for those States to improve their mental health systems. Victoria had spent the money wisely and had reported improved outcomes. NSW, on the other hand, had hoarded its grant, and the mental health system had languished, to say the least. For the last few years, it was obvious that the system was now terrible, and a number of official Enquiries asked to what extent it was in trouble and pondered on why. In September, a Royal Commission on this matter was due to report.

The central focus of the Commission was on Callan Park, in Sydney's inner western suburbs. This provided residential accommodation for patients from all over the State, and was the showpiece of the NSW system. As the Commission progressed, person after person pointed out weaknesses of this institution, and finally the Superintendent, Dr Bailey, agreed with these observations and liberally poured scorn on the State Government, and many health professionals practising there. As a consequence, his position there was in jeopardy, and he resigned. The Commission reported almost immediately thereafter, and was highly critical of the system, from the involvement of the Government, right down to the treatment patients received in the wards.

The first Letter is a rebuff, by their Union Association, to various claims made against staff.

Letters, A Torkington, Hospital Employees' Assoc. of NSW, Sydney. It is now crystal clear that the allegations in the "Herald" articles and in Dr Bailey's report so far as the staff is concerned are false. The "Herald" claimed that "sections of the staff" were sadistic, that some attendants derived "warped satisfaction from the infliction of cruelty." In fact over a five-year period five men had been dismissed for assaults on four patients before the Commission was set up.

The Commissioner found one of these men had committed another assault in 1956, an attendant who had left the service some time before the "Herald" articles had committed two assaults, a patient had been hit for stealing and eating some food which would impair his health, and some boys in Male Ward 7 had been cuffed for stealing food. The "Herald" claimed that female staff were guilty of dishonesty and inhumanity. This was disproved.

It further claimed that "bold organized theft" was competently practiced by the male nursing staff. The Commissioner found that at this time there was, at the most, petty pilfering by some of the kitchen staff.

The "Herald" has not, regrettably, had the grace to apologise to the men and women it so sensationally and inaccurately vilified.

So far as Dr Bailey's report is concerned, it is apparent that it is dealing kindly with him to say his report was exaggerated. We regret that the Commission did not inquire into Dr Bailey's fitness for his position. We hope changes will be made at Callan Park. But since loyalty and co-operation and mutual confidence between staff and administration are necessary we believe that immediate consideration must be given to Dr Bailey's position.

Comment.   The weight of evidence, and indeed the findings of the Commission, **spoke strongly against this view.**

Letters, An Ex-RMO, Sydney. The Government grants to the hospitals were shockingly inadequate so the whole Departmental emphasis was on economy. The medical superintendents and business managers who rose in favour were those who ran their hospitals as cheaply as possible, and above all with no disturbing incidents to arouse trouble or criticism.

Whenever I, as a newcomer, came across incidents of neglect, ill-treatment or injury of patients, or of theft of the scanty luxuries in their food, as anyone did who kept his eyes and ears open; the advice of my colleagues always was, "Don't be a fool – forget it. **If you report it, every staff member will swear it isn't true, and the patients will be too intimidated to give evidence.** Anyhow, who will accept the evidence of people mentally deranged? If you force an inquiry, you'll fail to prove your case. You'll only succeed in stirring up enmity against yourself and make your own work very difficult. You'll do no good for the patients and the management certainly won't thank you for the unwelcome trouble and publicity you will stir up."

I had to accept the truth of this assessment of the situation although I did once succeed in getting the dismissal of a nurse who had made a vindictive and sadistic attack on a patient.

There has certainly been an improvement in the mental hospitals since my day, but Mr Justice McClemens' findings on the "wall of silence," and the reception that Dr Bailey is now receiving, make it quite clear that the old conditions and attitudes still exist.

It is only against this background that Dr Bailey's fearless stand can be adequately appreciated and fairly judged.

Letters, L Hanlon. So the pack is in full cry. The Hospital Employees' Union would like to see Dr Bailey digging salt in Siberia. Why? Are they vainly trying to cover up their own shortcomings by belittling a medical superintendent for trying to raise the standards of his hospital? This conglomeration of employees dares to dictate to the government upon the fate of a brave man!

If they had one ounce of Dr Bailey's courage and a grain of his intelligence they would try to clean up the mess in their own back yard instead of venting their rage and frustration upon the only person not guilty of the neglect and cruelty that pervades our mental hospitals.

This Union does not appear in a very good light. Is it trying to show any other reformer just what will happen to him if he dares to raise his voice against the perks apparently enjoyed by the hospital staff in the past?

Letters, T Lilley. What kind of mid-summer madness is rampant in our society when such a public benefactor as Dr Bailey is obliged to resign his position?

It was often thus with pioneers and reformers, and Dr Bailey has reaped censure where he should have received commendation. Have not his disclosures and the "Herald's" revelations resulted in a brighter prospect for the mentally ill? Is there not hope for eventual good where before there was a festering sore? The relatives of those who are, or who have been, in this Sate's mental hospitals should be clamorous in their support of Dr Bailey, who first set this stone a-rolling.

Comment. The State Government came out of this very badly. So too did many of the health professionals, and many of the practices that they used. For example, psychiatrists and their prolific use of shock therapy came under criticism.

The end result was that the NSW mental health system got a jolt, and jumped forward for a few years. That had to be welcomed. And other States at various times got their jolts too. But the end result, now in 2021, is that mental health is still the impoverished cousin of general health, and that many more jolts will be needed to bring it up to parity, and up to scratch.

BIKINIS IN THE NEWS

The weather in Sydney last weekend was terrific. Plenty of sun, no wind, and so a perfect day for the beach. Thousands of surfers trundled out to places like Bondi and Manly, and set up there for a day of sunburn and sand rash. It was one of those perfect fun-filled days.

On Bondi, however, it turned out differently for 50 young belles. Because there, the Chief Inspector, Mr Laidlaw, was offended by the fact that they had appeared in bikinis, some of them offensive, and some "rolled down", and he insisted that they leave the beach. He said at the time "I do not want to see offensive costumes on the beach. At the end of last season, they were getting pretty bad, but this year they have now gone too far."

Next day, after sending three more girls home, he said "there is no arbitrary line that can be drawn in making judgments. After you have been on the beach for a while, you know what's right and what isn't."

He pointed out that beach costumes were regulated by a 1935 ordinance. It demanded that both men's and women's costumes must have legs at least three inches long. They must completely cover the front of the body from a line at the level of the armpits to the waist. Cover the front, back and side of the body from the waist to the end of the three-inch legs, and have shoulder straps. They must also have a half skirt covering the front of the body from the waist to the end of the leg coverings.

The various authorities were quick to say that, officially, the 1935 Ordinance would no longer be enforced. But that still left a great deal to the sensitivities of people like beach inspectors. In any case, the general public had a few views on the matter.

Letters, B Foggon. The "Herald" is to be congratulated on its sub-editorial "Beaches And

Bikinis", which pointed out the need for an up-to-date ordinance on beach attire.

In the meantime it is to be hoped that beach inspectors pay more attention to men's wear, which is often much more questionable than women's. Whatever the merits of bikinis as still further abbreviated (and on this there could be something in the French saying, "Indecency begins where beauty ends"), they could never be so ugly, offensive and untidy as Vs worn by men – particularly fat men.

Letters, Louis Segol Let me say what **does** offend me on our beaches: filthy people who strew rubbish everywhere, uncontrolled larrikins and people who allow their dogs to run uncontrolled on the beach to offend on clothing.

The larrikins crowd adjacent beer gardens and throw lewd remarks at every young woman who passes and make life unbearable with their yells; they camp and drink and sleep all night on the beach with their girls and leave their bottles, often broken for the ratepayers to have removed; they make the night hideous with their car horns and open exhausts, and disturb the peace of other sunbathers by their uncouth behavior.

Bikinis, when worn, as they mostly are, by attractive, healthy young misses, cannot be said to offend if we are honest about it. If occasionally they go beyond the realm of decency they can easily be controlled by the beach inspectors at Bondi or anywhere else.

These young women seem to be very quiet on the beaches, which cannot be said of many of the young males, whose scanty trunks must often offend the womenfolk more.

Letters, L Hellyer. With the approach of the swimming season, it is to be hoped that beach inspectors and other authorities will give some attention to the banning of the bikini and other offensive bathing gear.

There would be very few indeed who would wish a strict enforcement of the local government laws in regard to the design of costumes, but in the pre-bikini state I feel that a reasonable compromise had been reached between the law and decency. Since no excuse can be found for the bikini on the grounds of appearance, health or comfort, it is reasonable to assume that it appeals to those exhibitionists who always wish to be a little more "daring" than their fellows.

When will women realize that there is nothing very attractive about the female navel?

Letters, John Robert. Now that the annual bikini wrangle is in full swing it may be appropriate to ask, "Is the human form as revealed by the bikini really indecent?"

One may reasonably see the advent of mixed bathing in brief attire as a welcome advancement towards ridding society of it self-imposed stigma. But not if well-meaning but misguided beach inspectors and others have a say in the matter. Their efforts only focus the attention of innocent children upon this intangible phenomenon, "indecency".

In the final analysis the bikini question will no doubt be considered not as an issue of morals or decency, but merely as a matter of taste. If all that offended taste in one way or another was banned we would have little left of anything.

Letters, Kathleen Mathews. It amazes me to read that we need beach inspectors and special ordinances to force our women to wear a certain size swimming costume to public beaches.

I would feel sure that our girls would have enough modesty and respect for themselves to be their own censors.

We have the honour to be born of the "fairer sex" and the wonderful power to inspire in our menfolk noble feelings of protectiveness, wholesomeness, respect and admiration – and bikinis won't do that.

Remember, bikini belles. You may one day have fine sons of your own and will want them to walk our beautiful beaches proud and glad of the lovely, modest girls they see there.

Letters, J Sheppard, Bondi Beach. As a bikini wearer – and far from being in my first youth – I take considerable umbrage at being dubbed by L H Hellyer either an "exhibitionist" or a would-be "daring" character.

I wear a bikini because I find it more comfortably by reason of the freedom from pull and strain on the shoulders and legs, and also more healthful, since there is less wet costume clinging around the body, keeping out the sun and air, and aggravating a fibrositis tendency. Appearance and the "decencies" are observed by wearing a bikini which is conservative and well fitting. Although using the personal pronoun here I feel sure the above reasons must apply to many bikini wearers.

Letters, Clive Hart, Merewether. It seems to me that one of the things most seriously wrong with this otherwise splendid country is that its men fail to find beauty in a woman's navel.

Letters, (Mrs) Joan Wilson. Since the wearing of abbreviated costumes is, in the main, confined to teenagers, many of whom cannot be expected to know what constitutes good, decent and restrained behavior – and to males, whose proverbial looseness is well known – why not set aside some beach for the sole use of these semi-nudists? They are an eyesore, and an offence to all recognized principles of decency and to older, well-educated, well-balanced people.

There is an unfortunate tendency today to "play down" older and refined responsible citizens – who should be, and often try to be, the "teachers" of untrained youth. These citizens have a right to the sort of conditions on beaches which conform to recognized "decent" standards. Why should they daily be nauseated, and often forced to leave the beach, because of the highly irresponsible, disgusting and indecent behavior of a lot of half-naked, immodest young females and their male consorts who find it "modest" to appear half-naked before the general public?

The natives of South Africa and the Pacific Islands also bathe in the nude. Why not transport these young females and V-clad males to some such place, where they would be welcomed, and would not offend the tender susceptibilities of those coloured races who have not yet attained the higher standards of civilization, ethical behavior and common decency?

Letters, Naval Observer (Ret.).The bikini controversy seems to have reached the point where it is generally accepted that it is not the size or shape of the bikini that matters, but the size and shape of the wearer.

This being so, I suggest that the most obvious solution is that only those holding a current bikini licence (to be reviewed annually) should be allowed to wear a bikini in public.

Comment. For a few weeks the Ministers of Government made a lot of noise about writing a new Ordinance. But as they got more into the subject they realised how difficult it was. So, for the time being, it stayed put in the too-hard basket, and the ladies were free to parade with gay abandon, if not full abandon.

A POM HOMEWARD BOUND

An Englishman, writing as **Homeward Bound**, wrote a long Letter in which he gave Australia a very poor report card. I have taken an edited excerpt and reproduced it below. His Letter brought forth many responses, and I provide a sample below.

He wrote that Letters and articles appearing in the "*Herald*" provide the answers to a question often asked: "Why do so many English migrants return to England just as soon as the opportunity presents itself? I have given my reasons below."

He went on to talk about a number of political incidents that had been in the news recently. He mentioned a few occasions when the White Australia Policy had been applied. He said that the transport system and our buses were the worst in the world, and that the employees were the rudest. He found the treatment of animals here disgusting. The NSW Government's reaction to the Callan Park revelations were typical and turned his stomach. He pointed out that Englishmen were not welcome, but the Catholics from Italy and Ireland were.

He went on to say that "there are more important things than nice weather. In a few weeks, I hope to leave here for the rainy but comparatively safe shores, of England. Such real fears I have of your security police, and of your police in general, that I ask you not to publish my name".

Letters, A Fatseas. There is a Greek adage that "Whoever is born in prison, he will ever remember prison." This means that even prison is a home to those who are born in it. I am reminded of this proverb every time discouraged migrants find it necessary to blast the "appalling" conditions in this country and publicise their return home.

A classical example of such incurably disgruntled people is the anonymous Englishman, "Homeward Bound," whose impulsion to give up Australia has been intensified by such matters as the case of the two Malayans, the treatment of animals in Australia, the Brenner case, the Callan Park scandal, the transport service.

With the exception of the last matter (some bus conductors do need a lesson or two in courtesy), his list of causes is so extraneous to his immediate personal interests and welfare that it reveals the same flimsy line of defence taken up by all those over-nostalgic and presumptuous people whose kind should never migrate. They find nothing as good as their own, and in fact they delight in saying so. They expect privileges and concessions, for they believe they have made sacrifices in coming here.

The fact that Australia is obliged only to provide work and not grant distinctions to certain classes of migrants, be they Britons, former war allies, or former enemies, be they Protestants, Roman Catholics or atheists, is seen by these people as a conspiracy in which preferential treatment is meted out.

Letters, S Smith. I have just returned to Australia after spending several years in England, and I would like to warn "Homeward Bound" that he is not likely to find his own country quite the Utopia he is picturing it from so many miles away. He has no doubt forgotten all the irritations which caused him to migrate.

Letters, T Harding. As an Englishman, I would like to show the other side of the picture according to my experience of Australia.

I arrived here with my wife and four children in 1948, since when we have enjoyed greater health and prosperity than ever in our lives before. Three of the children are now married to Australians and, besides owning their own homes and cars, enjoy incomes in the 2,000 Pounds-a-year bracket. The unmarried one also has a car and a comparable income.

These results were not achieved wholly unaided, but partly though the help of warmhearted and kindly Australians who were unknown to us before we arrived. During the abovementioned period I have revisited the "old country" on three occasions, and each time the general deterioration in conditions, particularly with regard to taxation, seems to be greater. Crimes of violence are so rampant that a large section of the community has recently made strong representation to the Government for the reintroduction of flogging and an extension for the law governing capital punishment.

Unlike "Homeward Bound" I am not afraid to publish my name, or to say, "Thank you, Australia".

Letters, D Anthony. The following, based on personal experiences in England, provide the answer to a question often asked: "Why do nearly all Australian visitors to England return home as soon as they have had a good look around?"

One. Fear for their safety in many such vicinities as Notting Hill Gate, where the coloured colonial is given a "fair go".

Two. While they appreciate the courtesy extended to them by the same coloured colonial transport employees, little can be said for the churlish attendants at most country railway stations.

Three. Figures published in the London Press show cases of cruelty to children to be far in excess of those cruelty to animals. Also, frenzied animal worship extends so far as to refusals of invitations because of inability to obtain a sitter for "mummy's darling little pooch". Cruelty to animals in the form of "riding the hounds" is, of course, reserved for the elite.

Four. The lack of such men as Mr Downer. With him at the helm, English Security would surely have screened the likes of the Continental gentlemen who set up their vice empire in the West End. Australians have no stomach for apathy towards security, whether moral or national.

Letters, H Bennet-Wood, Sec. UK Services and Ex-Services Welfare Association, Sydney. Homeward Bound's letter is unfortunate, as it must react unfavourably on British migrants who are anxious to settle happily in their new environment.

There is no space to consider the complaints put forward, but I feel impelled to say that, after 20 years' residence here, I have never experienced any lack of courtesy from the employees of the Department of Road Transport.

It is true that in some respects the British migrant is at a disadvantage. This often arises because the United Kingdom authorities have no "consular powers", this being a British country. For example, migrants from Italy, thanks to their Government's interest, not only receive help with their housing problems, but are now getting substantial help in their difficulties arising from prolonged unemployment.

Any British migrant who has secure employment and a home can settle happily here, and the great majority do so. Unfortunately, the housing and employment positions are both extremely bad and seem likely to remain so. That is the salient reason why so many good British families are "homeward bound".

Letters, Douglas Reeve. A disgruntled migrant, faced with the prospect of spending hundreds of pounds in fares, naturally wishes to justify, if only to himself, his inability to adjust, but why not go quietly without making such a fuss about it? It sounds so much like a small boy who shouts rude remarks over his shoulder as he runs away.

As another English migrant who has come to love this happy, sunny land, may I wish this bitter, bigoted gentleman "bon voyage, good riddance, and may the secret police please not hinder his departure."

SOME NEWS ITEMS

The Federal Minister for National Resources announced that **iron ore deposits** had been newly discovered in vast areas of Western Australia.

Talks between China and the US over **South Vietnam** have reached an impasse. It was feared in America that Communist infiltration of the South might need to be checked by forceful means.

Adolf Eichmann, Hitler's slayer of Jews, was sentenced to death. There was never any doubt about this decision.

Blood tests for alcohol-in-motorists were getting serious consideration in all States. **TARAX** reported a big increase in sales so far this summer.

Tanya Verstack is Miss Australia for the year.

Australian firms are reporting that trials of selling **bottled and canned water** are going well, and there is a prospect that the product might be introduced on a permanent basis.

Fishing licences for amateur fishermen are being proposed in several States. Amateur fishing bodies across the nation are being asked to combine to meet this threat to their rightful recreation.

Rent controls on NSW properties are under review. They cover all dwellings existing in 1939, and these have seen no increase in rental from that date. This had been of great value to tenants. To remove the controls would see rents increase enormously, and tenants would be well out of pocket. On the other hand, the freezing of rents has been unfair to landlords for decades. This will be a huge political issue.

THE WORLD WAS STILL AT IT

More headlines taken from a single day, October 31st'. From a single paper, the *SMH*, on a normal day.

CALL UP OF TROOPS IN BRITAIN. The UK wanted support over Germany "crisis".

WEST CONCERN OVER SOVIET–POLAND DEMAND. More diplomatic posturing.

BRITAIN MAY BE FIRST TARGET IN NUCLEAR WAR. It makes a good story, though often-told.

DEMAND IN UN FOR SANCTIONS ON SOUTH AFRICA. Everyone wanted to boycott South Africa.

"TERROR BOMB" CONDEMNATION. Russia was back detonating bigger and bigger bombs.

"DEATH LAWS" IN GHANA. Martial law, and no law, had been introduced, and imposed in an arbitrary fashion.

TENSION RISES IN ALGERIA. Overnight, 60 plastic bombs were exploded in the city of Algiers.

H-BOMB FALLOUT – NO CAUSE FOR ALARM. Good news for Australia, from Professor Titterton.

STRIKE DRAGS ON IN MT ISA. What else would you expect? Well-thought-out strikes were always most effective in the run-up to Christmas.

MAN DIES TO SAVE CATS IN FIRE. Just a reminder that more prosaic news sometimes turned up as well.

NOVEMBER: ABORIGINES IN THE NEWS

Aborigines politically had seen a quiet year, with no major initiatives passed by the Legislatures. But all evidence pointed to the fact that public sympathy was moving more in their direction, and that bold moves would receive widespread support. In fact, next year, that support was given, and Queensland and Western Australia and Northern Territory conceded that Aborigines had the right to vote in State elections. Then, in NSW, the prohibition on their access to alcohol was removed.

I know that these changes were **only part of a much bigger whole**, and that plenty more changes were needed. I also know that these were concessions granted at the macro level, and that is **very different from gaining equality at the personal level.** Still, they were steps in the right direction, and were a clear and definite sign that white people were becoming aware of the maltreatment handed out by society to the blacks, and were ready to act for change.

Another issue relating to Aborigines was raised in a Letter.

Letters, J O'Brien. In recent articles and correspondence in the "Herald", casual mention has been made of a matter that seems to be worthy of closer attention: the alleged assertion by white children that they are offended by the odour of Aborigines.

During the last war, I served within Australia and was ultimately assigned to work connected with Courts-martial. Numerous soldiers brought before the Courts-martial, on charges of being absent without leave, were Aborigines or part-castes, and in practically every instance the excuse offered for their offence was that the white soldiers would not mix with them, but no specific reason was ever tendered for this.

Many of these Courts-martial, in which Aboriginal soldiers were concerned, were presided over by an officer who, when pronouncing judgment, always ordered that the prisoner should be transferred to one specified battalion so that he might mingle with others of his own kind.

This officer knew the Aborigines well and had great sympathy for them, and one day he explained to me his real reason for always ordering the transfer of Aboriginal offenders to the battalion specified. He said (and I quote his own words as nearly as I can recollect them): "Take an Aboriginal or a part-caste, wash and scrub him until he is absolutely free of odour, array him in a new, unused uniform, and within 24 hours he will have developed a characteristic 'Aboriginal' odour."

I cannot speak to this, but some of your correspondents may be able to do so and, if the statement be correct, some research by competent investigators might produce results that could be to the benefit of Aborigines and aid in their assimilation, a result that I, for one, would heartily welcome.

Letters, Reg Mahoney. It was my privilege during the last war to spend some time right beside an Aboriginal soldier, who, to use the term of his mates, was "as black as your hat." But there was no cleaner man in the regiment and no suggestion of any complaints about odour whether characteristic or not.

I have no doubt that many more people would qualify for criticism if they lived in a tin humpy, as many of our Aborigines do, with a kerosene tin to serve as bathroom and laundry.

A practical approach to this problem would be to put a bulldozer through the tin humpies and encourage Aborigines to accept better standards of living and improved personal hygiene.

Letters, M Fox. From time to time lately we have had Aboriginal people, both men and women, staying with us in our small cottage. They have come either straight from reserves and stations, or from their own homes as far away as Brewarrina and Cairns. We have also visited Aboriginal people in their own environment in the country and the city, and can assure your correspondent, J O'Brien, that Aboriginal people have no odour distinct from that of white people.

As it happens, we have an Aboriginal woman staying with us at this very moment, and the strong odour of racial prejudice contained in Mr O'Brien's unscientific suggestion did much to ruin all our breakfasts.

Letters, D Leithhead. The "Aborigines' odour" problem cuts both ways. In the blistering summer of 1939, a party of us were kindly allowed to use the excellent shower-room at Hermansburg

Mission – priceless concession at that time and place, though the pervading odour was rather overpowering.

Strange to relate, few of the mission natives took their daily shower after we had finished ours. They couldn't stand the stink left by us.

Letters, Aboriginal Well-Wisher. I have read with interest the recent letters on Aboriginal odour. My husband and I for many years have been keen advocates of the assimilation of the Aboriginal into our community.

Some years ago, a religious body was interested in testing the effect of placing a talented Aboriginal child (not full-blood) in a normal home. As I had studied anthropology at Sydney University and as I, as a Christian, believed in the equality of races, the boy was offered a home with us for one year. The lad was extremely interested in sport and very good at both cricket and football. He therefore led an energetic life and perspired freely. But he bathed or showered twice a day and had more frequent changes of clothing than is the case with boys of his age. He always slept with his window wide open and that window remained open throughout the day except when weather conditions did not permit.

Although in our affection for the boy we never told him so, and therefore we now wish to remain anonymous, there was a distinct odour about his person and his room which was quite different from the odour of perspiration and which often became very nauseating. It is of fundamental importance to recognise that we whites had for the lad also a nauseating odour which the lad tried to explain to me.

The odour is as distasteful to the black as to the white. It is impossible to ignore that each race detects a nauseating odour in the other. If the Aborigines are to be assimilated, and that is the only solution to their problems, we must recognize this fact and strive scientifically to find means of alleviating it. In the meantime we must face the situation with love and understanding.

Letters, H Howe. Having lived among and worked with Aborigines and other coloured races for 30-odd years, I have frequently heard their opinions on the matter. Anyone who has worked with Aborigines or travelled through the bush with them will have noticed how persistently Binghi keeps to windward of his white companions. If asked why, he replies, "S'pose get down wind whitefeller too much stink."

Aboriginal children in our far northern schools often voice the same complaint. In hot weather, classes of piccaninny age usually have to be moved out of classrooms into the open air of the verandas or under the schoolhouse to do their lessons because they become nauseated by the body odour of their white classmates.

With crews composed of Malays, Japanese, Chinese, Filipinos and Aborigines, the question of body odour was of some importance in the confined space of pearling luggers.

Members of all of the above races were very
conscious of the body odour of other races,
but all found that of the white man the most
objectionable, with one exception – Binghi on a
hot day after a feed of alligator. He was never
allowed back on a lugger for 48 hours after such
a meal. Nothing on earth smells worse. Binghi's
fondness for 'gator meat is in fact one of the most
formidable barriers in the way of his assimilation
in the Territory and the Kimberleys.

MELBOURNE CUP, 1961

The papers were full of talk about horse-racing early in
November, and it appears that there was a racing Carnival
in Melbourne at the time. Apparently, this lasts for a week
or so, and the major event is called the Melbourne Cup.
Well, this year it was run again, and I can tell you that a
dark brown or black horse won it. Its name eludes me at
the moment, but if I tell you it was ridden by a very short
man in strange coloured clothing, and carrying a piccolo
with a tassle, you might work out the winner.

Be that as it may, it brought forth two interesting Letters.

Letters, S G Menser.   If the Davis Cup
can be played anywhere in the world, then
notwithstanding anything else contained in the
rules of racing, why can't the Melbourne Cup be
run in Sydney in 1962?

Speaking on behalf of many keen followers of the
sport, we are perfectly willing to allow the AJC to
transfer the Sydney Cup to Melbourne next year
(very few Sydneysiders see it) and of course we
would willingly throw in The Metropolitan.

It seems only just that Sydney should be delighted at the sight of so many magnificent animals. Surely Melbourne will be gracious enough to at least benefit our blighted eyes one day in 1962.

Letters, W T Ward. As an expatriate Melbournian I protest in shocked astonishment at the suggestion that the 1962 Melbourne Cup should be run in Sydney.

With pompous condescension he offers the transfer of the "Sydney Cup" to Melbourne, together with The Metropolitan – the latter being apparently regarded as a "douceur".

Let me assure him that if he were to offer the Waratah Festival, Bondi Beach and the leading classic of Wentworth Park in addition, it would not avail him in the slightest.

To think that Sydney, having been endowed with its Harbour, its Hawkesbury, its Beaches and its Bridge, and **having sullied them all**, should now turn its beady, covetous eyes on the Melbourne Cup, will make the hard core of fair-minded natives, which I am convinced it still possesses, again bow their heads in shame.

The Melbourne Cup, like the opening day of Ascot, will never be held in Sydney. More in sorrow than in anger, I deplore the fact that it has ever been suggested in Sydney that it should.

HIGH COST OF DYING

For a few weeks, there had been a lot of commentary about the funeral industry, and the mysterious ways in which it went about its business, and how it assessed its cost. In early October, a well-known funeral director made a statement that said all of **his** charges for services were legitimate, but that cut-price operators were cutting corners and lowering standards. This opened the way for the following Letters, which provide quite interesting views of the industry back then.

Letters, W Johnson. I would like R V Kinsela, who attacked so-called cheap funeral operators, to know that the public is over-charged by funeral directors to a great extent. It's high time the Government made a thorough investigation of the costs and service given by them.

Letters, (Rev.) John Campbell. It is well known that the ministrations of clergymen at the time of bereavement present powerful opportunities for bringing comfort and for evangelism: to show that, for those who love Jesus Christ, death is not the end but the beginning. But in many ways, the undertakers of this city have sought to undermine or take away from clergymen these opportunities. It is rare for the undertaker to consult a rector before fixing the time and place of a funeral, and it has been my experience that the parish clergyman is sometimes the very last person to be informed.

Some of the private chapels established by undertakers are pleasantly furnished, but others are objectionable in the extreme. Frequently they leave the coffin open in such chapels until just before the service. Coloured spotlights shine on the face of the corpse, and sickly sentimental recorded music is invariably played.

I have been astounded to discover the shockingly high prices charged by some undertakers. Many of them demand a 50 per cent deposit on the day the funeral is ordered, and complete settlement within a few days of the funeral. They are known to show their most expensive fitments first to bereaved relatives, knowing that such relatives will not be in a fit state to demand anything cheaper. Such callous behavior deserves censure, and there is thus an urgent need for a law-enforced code of ethics for undertakers.

Letters, Leslie Andrews. As a person, who, with the temerity of youth, rented a simple little shop and with the barest necessities opened a funeral business, which has endured and grown for 24 years, permit me to defend the right of the small man so to continue, untrammeled by the ever-growing mass of red tape which is increasingly shackling the vitality of all enterprise.

Over the years I have noticed that the desire to stifle competition has been the mainspring of the wish of the funeral directors for licensing. The big businessmen, surrounded by the accretions of inefficiency which grow with the years, have no desire for keener competition. They would have it believed that funeral work is complex instead of relatively simple. The bureaucrat, wishing to expand his empire, fosters a similar belief.

May I also be permitted to comment on the paucity of arguments put forward by the Rev.

John F S Campbell in support of his accusation of malpractice. Some funeral directors may not be delicate in their financial approach, but be it remembered they have to carry bad debts in the case of which **no goods can be repossessed** to mitigate their impact. Even Government funeral-benefit cheques, which peculiarly are made payable **to the person arranging the funeral,** not the funeral director, are sometimes never received by the funeral director.

Letters, C Hewit, Cremation Society of Australia. Some people who, for religious or other reasons, are opposed to cremation frequently make irresponsible statements covering procedure either for the purpose of creating doubt in the minds of the public or offending the finer feelings of those who have been so unfortunate as to require the services of funeral directors or cremation authorities.

The statement made by Mr Charles Meeking, that he **understands coffins are re-used**, shows either malice or ignorance. Your newspaper is, of course, seeking facts, which leads us to say without reservation and unequivocally that his remarks are completely untrue.

Not in any circumstances are funeral directors or any other persons permitted to remove coffins or fittings from crematoria and they are consumed without interference by the same incandescent heat that reduces the human remains to their final indestructible elements.

The statement has the unqualified support of all seven authorities in New South Wales, whose operations are subject to inspection under the Public Health Act by the Department of Health.

Letters, Accountant. Years ago, even before funeral costs were at the present astronomical height, I overcame this problem of expense (and mourning) by willing my body to Sydney University, and I have its acceptance in writing. This serves a dual purpose, as in addition to the aforementioned reason, there is the great opportunity to further medical science, which should be a thought paramount in our minds at all times.

I, as others, deplore the high cost of any kind of funeral, the expenses of which, as obviously is the view of the Federal Taxation department, should not be more than the 30 Pounds allowed as a deduction under (mostly rare) certain circumstances.

Comment. Since 1961, funerals have become a lot more expensive, in real terms, and a lot more elaborate. Here, though, I would like to direct attention briefly to another essential part of life where costs have almost gotten out of hand. Namely, wedding costs. Just take the reception. Back then, it was often curried egg or cooked ham sandwiches with pickles, cakes cooked by the neighbours, trifle from a few aunties, an ice cream cake for the kids, a keg of beer in the back room of the church hall, followed by a waltz and then an old time dance. Perhaps with a jazz waltz and quickstep thrown in. This was all topped off by the three tiered wedding cake, with white icing, made by Mrs Grahame down the street, who always did a really good job on these.

Today it is different. You all know how expensive it has become. I'm not sure that the result has been any better.

SCRIPTURE IN SCHOOLS

Letters, C Dean-Dickey. The Anglican Synod last week passed a resolution urging the State Government to include passages or books of scripture as studies in the examinations in English for the Intermediate and Leaving certificates.

One feels that this is as fresh and forward approach to the study of scripture in our schools. I am at a loss to understand the custom of including the work of an Elizabethan poet and playwright as the principal study in English, even if his name was William Shakespeare. There is so much of the Bible which can be studied purely as literature, and which at the same time can convey a deeper moral and spiritual value to the adolescent mind than any selection from the Bard of Avon.

Those who are successful in their Leaving Certificate, and particularly those who go on to university, can be regarded as the future leaders of our land. But can anyone claiming to be educated who is without a knowledge of God, without even the rudiments of a Christology, and without a knowledge of the part that the Christian Church has played in our history?

DECEMBER ELECTION RESULTS

On December 9th the nation went to the polls. The Liberal and Country Parties between them had a House majority of 16 seats, and despite the credit squeeze they had introduced and mismanaged, they looked certain of another victory. Bob Menzies, and his Treasurer, Harold Holt, were both masters of standing on their records, and promising nothing more definite than **more jobs and increased prosperity**. So they were not proposing policy initiatives or any shake-ups or changes. Business as usual.

The Labor Party was in the hands of two very different people. The Leader, Arthur Calwell, was one of the old school of socialists and, as my father used to say, had one of the best Union brains of **the 19th Century**. His Deputy, Gough Whitlam, was up-and-coming, and anxious to effect changes in society a long way from the more prosaic interests of Calwell. Calwell however dominated election coverage, and his policy was to promise **more jobs and increased prosperity**. On the policy front, this election was a write-off.

As you might expect, television was used more and more by both major Parties, though the old-style barn-storming Town Hall meetings were still in vogue. Both leaders commonly attracted crowds of 1,000 at major cities, and these provided a lot of heat and no light, as usual. Menzies excelled at jousting with vocal opponents, and usually got the upper hand over them. Calwell was much less able, but his meetings were quite carefully stacked to lessen the venom of attacks. On television, their appearances were about as drab as is possible.

Immediately after the election, the Liberals and Menzies were jubilant. They appeared to have lost only six seats, and this was a better showing than they had expected. But as the week wore on, and straggling voters came in, the numbers went more and more against them. At one stage, it looked like Labor might win, then it looked like a hung parliament, but finally it ended up with the Libs holding office by two seats.

Comment. Most commentators agree that Menzies did not win this election. Labor failed to take a prize thrust upon it. If Labor and Calwell had enunciated policies, any policies, for social change, they would have been swept in. But they did not. So they stayed in Opposition, and in fact stayed there for about another decade.

LAST WORD ON VENDING MACHINES

Letters, J Stewart, Service Station Assoc. of NSW, North Sydney. The big majority of service-station operators are small businessmen who could not possibly afford the 1,200 to 1,300 Pounds required to buy a self-service pump and to have it installed. For those who could afford this cost, it just would not be an economic proposition if more than a dozen or so of these machines were operating in, say, a district the size of the Sydney metropolitan area.

As far as service to the public is concerned, how many drivers really want to buy petrol outside the legal trading hours? If the public can buy other commodities every bit as essential as petrol in the five-and-a-half-day, 50-hour retail stores trading week, why can't it buy its petrol in the seven-day, 94½ hour trading week worked by service stations?

Mention has been made for the efficacy of self-service pumps in other States, particularly Victoria. It is significant that the number of such pumps operating in Victoria has remained relatively very small. Also, those who claim that self-service pumps would eliminate illegal after-hours trading have obviously not studied the Victorian scene.

After-hours trading has reached alarming proportions in that State, and in the Industrial Court, Melbourne, recently, no fewer than 50 service-station operators were convicted for late trading on one day! Many of these operators gave as an excuse the fact that a self-service pump was operating in their area and, because they could not afford one themselves, they were forced to continue trading beyond the legal trading hours.

Letters, N Arena. In answer to J D Stewart, Secretary of the Service Station Association of NSW, I would like to point out that the big majority of service station operators are not small businessmen in the sense Mr Stewart implies, but **lessees of the oil companies**. Does Mr Stewart really believe that the oil companies cannot afford 1,200 Pounds or less, per unit, to purchase automatic pumps for their service stations?

Secondly, I find it very hard to understand why the public can purchase from vending machines after legal trading hours chocolates, chewing-gum, postage stamps, coffee and cigarettes, but not an essential commodity, namely petrol

In answer to the question of how many drivers really want to buy petrol outside legal trading hours Mr Stewart, or anyone else interested, could be supplied with lists of names, addresses and signatures of drivers who signed a petition from every service station with an automatic petrol pump in the metropolitan area.

Comment. This matter had developed into a scandal. The NSW Government was pandering to the Trade Unions, and refusing to accept technological change. The paucity of Mr Stewart's argument is emphasised when you realize that the very fact that so many drivers were being fined for after-hours trading was a sign that there was a big demand for the machines. But a Government that had been in power for over 20 years was still confident that it could hold its place next time round, and so defied the clearly expressed will of the people. Incidentally, it was to good avail, because at the next elections, early in 1962, it won its way back into power again.

MY LAST WORD ON ABORIGINES

I had intended not to say anything more on Aborigines, but a Letter in December from a young girl changed my resolve. In thinking about Aborigines back in 1961, I expect most people often focused on tribal groups, in outback conditions, that were often marked by deprivation, violence, and perhaps drunkenness. But here we had a Letter from a completely different source, and it made me, 60-plus years later, sit up and take notice.

Letters, Careena. Schooldays are over and most of us are looking forward to a career, or some form of employment. To most young people this is an exciting time – our teacher referred to it as "the time of opportunity."

It is not a time of opportunity for me because there is no opportunity for people with a mixture of Aboriginal blood in their veins. I am only slightly coloured and at school was accepted and had many white friends, but already I know that my colour is a handicap and that inevitably I can expect to languish at home, day in and day out, just as many of my older coloured friends have done and are doing right now.

Every effort I make to improve myself will be frustrated. I shall apply for positions for which I know I am suited, but will receive the same negative reply as my friends have received. We are not wanted. From discussions with my family I learn that never have girls with Aboriginal blood held a position in Coff's Harbour; never have they been given the opportunity to show their worth and ability in the business community.

I need work to be able to maintain myself, to keep my dignity and self-respect. **I cry myself to sleep at night when I think of the hopelessness of myself and my people.** Is it any wonder other young Aboriginal people are embittered and genuinely despise the system which can keep us virtually in bondage?

Discrimination and apartheid are very evident here. My father himself says we are second-rate citizens with very few human rights.

The Aboriginal reserve, only two miles from town, is without electricity in AD 1961. We blame the Aborigines' Welfare Board for this, because we know the County Council has advised them that electricity connections can be made as soon as the Board gives its sanction.

How can children learn to live decently when day ends with darkness? Homework and constructive education are impossible until we have light.

Time only will tell if my melancholy outlook on life is warranted or otherwise. All I, and many of my coloured friends want, is opportunity.

Comment. Careena's Letters brought dozens of responses, all of them sympathetic. Many of them contained remedies, and only some of these were sensible. Nevertheless, they once again showed that there was an increasing percentage of the population who felt that Aborigines deserved better.

Another Letter suggested that every employer of any size take an Aboriginal onto their work force, and "they will soon be assimilated." The Writer of this Letter, from Burwood in Sydney, added that he was writing to Careena to offer her a job. Woolworths in Coffs Harbour chipped in and said it was now going to offer five jobs in its local stores for Aborigines.

Comment. I want to end this particular discussion by pointing out that right round the world, blacks were in violent revolt against their own repression. For example, in South Africa, Ghana, and the US. In all those places, concessions were gradually being wrung from the powers-that-be. We were seeing none of that violence here, and yet there was a perceptible change occurring in public opinion and this would soon lead to some improvements. As I look ahead, right up to the present, and I compare our **peaceful dreadfully-slow progress** with the **dreadfully-slow progress attained elsewhere by non-stop violence**, I scratch my head and wonder just how effective the violence has been and is.

RELIGION IN JOB SEEKING

I mentioned earlier that religion was clearly on the decline in society. Twenty years previously, it had been everywhere, ten years ago it appeared less, but now, it seemed that it had gone from public display and was hiding in the churches. But, in the workplace, it still lingered on, as the following exchanges indicate.

Letters, M Feeney. I have applied for jobs at various factories recently and one of the questions asked on the application forms is "What is your religion?"

I would like to know what is the connection between the way you do your job and religion.

Letters, A H Brown. M Feeney wants to know the connection between the way you do your job and religion.

Any business executive who is looking in a prospective employee for initiative, new ideas and capacity to shoulder responsibilities **cannot find these qualities of character** in a person whose religion indicates that he is content to let religious institutions control and mould his intellectual powers, within the limits prescribed by dogmatic theologians.

Letters, Employer. Your correspondent asks why employers sometimes ask an applicant's religion. It is for the same reason that we ask for particulars of education and experience and character references, and sometimes arrange for psychological tests of personality and aptitudes. If a man's religion means anything at all to him it should mean not merely sectarian partisanship, but a measure of moral education likely to develop qualities such as consideration for others.

Some acquire this without committing themselves to any denominational allegiance, and such would not be passed over by any reasonable employer. Nevertheless, religious training means something, and as an employer with a respect for the moral teachings of all the main Churches, I like to have a well-balanced staff of tolerant people drawn from all of them.

Letters, (Rev.) Gordon Powell. A considerable proportion of any clergyman's time is taken up writing character references for members of his congregation because the majority of employers are wise enough to know that a vital faith in God is the best guarantee of honesty, reliability, co-operation with others and many other qualities which they seek primarily in employees.

Comment. These last two Letters make it all seem as if the job market was ever so civilised. It was not, if I might say so. In many areas of the economy, there is no doubt that religion played a large part in getting a job. There were pockets in professions where being a Mason was a pre-requisite, and branches of the railways where being a Catholic was highly regarded, and in nursing where any non-Catholic was a shoe-in. Granted, there were many other areas where it seemed more equitable, but still most bosses did want to know your religion, and it is hard to believe that every one of them always used the info properly.

LAST CHANCE TO GRIZZLE

Now I will give oneLetter writer a last chance to vent his spleen about whatever it is that bugs him.

Letters, R Snow.   Could any of your readers let me know where I may obtain possession of a disused gaol? I am willing to swap my three-bedroom home in a "good class" suburb for vacant and sole possession of a gaol with high, strong walls. I wish to live in it myself to escape the attentions of other people's marauding children.

Within the walls of such a sanctuary, I hope to install a garden with flowers and fruit-trees, shady fish-ponds and other aids to quiet, relaxed outdoor living with my friends.

Such an inoffensive life is at present impossible for me because of parents who allow young children to roam at will through the grounds of any houses in the district.

Since the police cannot act against such youngsters, and since **no parent nowadays**

would dream of punishing his own child for anything whatever, the only course of action for me is to go and live in a place which has the protection of solid, unscalable walls.

So, please, any gaols for sale?

SUMMING UP 1961

I read these grizzles, and I look back on the major Oz issues of the year. Then I look at the that I gave you during this book. There is no comparison. Right across the world, in country after country, there was some sort of violent physical conflict, or serious threat of conflict. If not that, then there was the threat of atomic fallout or the real fear of nuclear oblivion. In other places, not reported, there was famine or plague.

When measured on an international scale, our own problems were dwarfed, **our own people were secure, and our property was sacrosanct.** That sounds like a pretty fair deal to me.

That will not, of course, stop me or you from grizzling. Fair enough. I suppose the issue that left me most deflated in the course of the year was the Callan Park enquiry.

I had a direct personal interest there. My elder brother, a beautiful young man with a small family, was caught in a fall of coal in a coal-mine. He was mainly buried for hours and came out with many fractures and a squashed head. When supposedly fixed up by the mining company doctor, he was told to go down the pit again. He could not do that.

The company then said he needed psychiatric help, and he was sent to Callan Park. There he was forcibly given multiple doses of electro-convulsive therapy, and was drugged out of all sensibility. He escaped, and arrived home on the run from police and warders. Our family and friends hid him till the authorities gave up looking six weeks later. This Callan Park experience haunted him till he died.

So, you will understand, I had my own little grizzle for the year. I bet that you, or your parents, also had their own sets of things they would like to change. But, I return to my earlier theme, that when seen in the larger picture, **they were small by comparison with the rest of the world.**

For the future, in terms of international politics, it is certain that whatever the US did, we would be dragged into it. We no longer followed the Brits, we were firmly on the American coat-tails. Soon enough, as you all know, we ended up fighting in Vietnam because of this. **I scratch my head and wonder what that bit of violence achieved.**

In the US, the space-race was, of now, definitely on the agenda. The US had been so smug about its progress in space that the Russian flights round the moon last year, and the feat of Yuri Gagaran this year, had left them in disarray. The race was really on, and so at the end of the decade, a man stepped onto the moon.

Locally, we still had our problems in **West New Guinea**. There is no doubt that Indonesia was genuine in its argument for possession of that land and, in its quest to form a new nation, was probably as much entitled to it as anyone else. The trouble was that there were no rules for deciding such hairy issues, and no one would abide by them even if there were. So it would all come down to who pawed at the ground most fiercely and who could pile up the biggest set of friendly bulls ready to butt. There were still a lot of headlines left in West Irian.

I thought that 1961 was notable for the emergence of **women and Aborigines** as political issues. Compared to a year ago, the press and political coverage they got this year was greatly increased, and the maturity of the matters discussed increased. It was noticeable, for women, that there was an increase in the proportion of serious Letters, with well thought-out themes and arguments, compared to the simple point-scoring Letters of previous years. These trends continued with gusto from here throughout the 1960's.

So here we are, at the end of 1961. It is a pity we could not have had more time together, but a parsimonious editor stopped that. For me, it was quite a good year in writing. Half a dozen times, I got tears in my eyes. And then, half a dozen times again, I stood up ready to punch someone on the nose. Compared to 1941, that was peace indeed.

In 1961, the contrast between **pacific Australia** and the rest of the troubled world was outstanding. At that time, almost alone in the world, I am happy to say that we in Australia enjoyed that most priceless boon, **security in our beds.** So now, all you 1961-ers, I bid you well, and I sincerely trust that **the security that we have had since then will continue for ever.**

In 1964, Stamp collecting was disappearing as a hobby, wine was no longer plonk, and mothers were waging war on old-fashioned tuck-shops. (God bless them. The tuck-shops, not the mothers). The Beatle cult was angering some people. The Tab: to be on not to be? Can true Reds get fat? Did Billie Graham have lasting effects? Prostitution was proposed as a safety valve against rape. Judy Garland got bad Press in Melbourne and left Oz in a sulk.

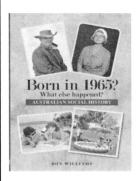

In 1965. Is the woman's place in the home? Winston Churchill died. Maybe we should cancel Anzac Day marches because of heavy drinking. Freedom Rides were exposing the treatment of Aborigines. Hemlines are going up, exposing "spiritual knees and legs". Dawn Fraser took the flag in Japan, the first Mavis Bramston Show was staged. Alphabet soup was filling bowls, and school projects were irritating corporations.

These 34 soft-cover books are available from:
www.boombooks.biz
They cover the years from 1939 to 1972